GOD'S GOT THIS

TRUTHS ON GOD'S SOVEREIGNTY FROM THE BOOK OF ESTHER

PAUL CHAPPELL

All Scripture quotations are taken from the King James Version.
Special emphasis in verses is added.

First published in 2022 by Striving Together Publications, a ministry of Lancaster Baptist Church, Lancaster, CA 93535. Striving Together Publications is committed to providing tried, trusted, and proven books that will further equip local churches to carry out the Great Commission. Your comments and suggestions are valued.

Striving Together Publications
4020 E. Lancaster Blvd.
Lancaster, CA 93535
800.201.7748

Edited by Monica Bass and Robert Byers
Cover design concept by Igniter Media

The author and publication team have put forth every effort to give proper credit to quotes and thoughts that are not original with the author. It is not our intent to claim originality with any quote or thought that could not readily be tied to an original source.

ISBN 978-1-59894-509-6 (paperback)
ISBN 978-1-59894-522-5 (ebook)

Printed in the United States of America

CONTENTS

ABOUT THIS STUDY GUIDE

Here is a brief explanation of the features of this study guide:

STUDY AND DISCUSSION A quick overview of the lesson as well as an outline is provided for your use as the group leader teaches through each study. You may find this material helpful to refer to as you review throughout the week.

DISCUSSION QUESTIONS Each lesson is complemented by a few thought-provoking questions to discuss with your group. These discussions can be rich times of learning from one another as you share insights and experiences.

DEVOTIONS There are five devotions—each with a Scripture passage and devotional reading—for each week of this study. These complement the lesson material and are designed to be read the week after the group leader presents the corresponding lesson.

REFLECT Each devotion ends by asking what God spoke to you about as you read the Scripture and devotion. This question is meant to encourage you to take a few moments to meditate on what you've read and ask the Lord to give you understanding and insight.

RESPOND This section gives you an opportunity to write down specific ways to apply the truths you are learning.

PRAY Each devotion concludes with a suggested prayer. You may find the written prayer provided helps you voice your heart to the Lord. Or you may choose to write or simply speak your own prayer as you communicate your heart to the Lord.

REMEMBER THE FORMER THINGS OF OLD: FOR I AM GOD, AND THERE IS NONE ELSE; I AM GOD, AND THERE IS NONE LIKE ME,

ISAIAH 46:9

WEEK ONE

GOD'S GOT THIS

DAY 1: God Is in Control

DAY 2: The Eternal King

DAY 3: God Has the Answers

DAY 4: Perfect Plans

DAY 5: God Never Forgets

WEEK ONE | STUDY AND DISCUSSION

GOD'S GOT THIS

Sometimes we feel overwhelmed or discouraged by the events of our lives or the wickedness surrounding us. Sometimes we feel as if God does not see or care—that He has forgotten us. The book of Esther assures us that the opposite is true. God does see, He does care, and He does have a plan.

As we study the book of Esther, we gain an amazing view of God's providence, goodness, and sovereignty always working on the behalf of His people—even when He is hidden from their view.

TEXT

For if thou altogether holdest thy peace at this time, then shall there enlargement and deliverance arise to the Jews from another place; but thou and thy father's house shall be destroyed: and who knoweth whether thou art come to the kingdom for such a time as this? (Esther 4:14)

INTRODUCTION

____

____

____

All nations before him are as nothing; and they are counted to him less than nothing, and vanity. (Isaiah 40:17)

Remember the former things of old: for I am God, and there is none else; I am God, and there is none like me, 10 Declaring the end from the beginning, and from ancient times the things that are not yet done, saying, My counsel shall stand, and I will do all my pleasure: (Isaiah 46:9–10)

1. HIS ____________________

I am Alpha and Omega, the beginning and the ending, saith the Lord, which is, and which was, and which is to come, the Almighty. (Revelation 1:8)

Quote: *"While there is no name of God, and no mention of the Hebrew religion anywhere, no one reads this book without being conscious of God."*
—G. Campbell Morgan

Quote: *"If the name of God is not here, His finger is."*—**Matthew Henry**

A. A Story of ____________________

Now it came to pass in the days of Ahasuerus, (this is Ahasuerus which reigned, from India even unto Ethiopia, over an hundred and seven and twenty provinces:) (Esther 1:1)

That saith of Cyrus, He is my shepherd, and shall perform all my pleasure: even saying to Jerusalem, Thou shalt be built; and to the temple, Thy foundation shall be laid. (Isaiah 44:28)

Quote: *"Providence is God's attention concentrated everywhere."*
—Augustus Strong

Now in the first year of Cyrus king of Persia, that the word of the LORD spoken by the mouth of Jeremiah might be accomplished, the LORD stirred up the spirit of Cyrus king of Persia, that he made a proclamation throughout all his kingdom, and put it also in writing, saying, 23 Thus saith Cyrus king of Persia, All the kingdoms of the earth hath the LORD God of heaven given me; and he hath charged me to build him an house in Jerusalem, which is in Judah. Who is there among you of all his people? The LORD his God be with him, and let him go up. (2 Chronicles 36:22–23)

The eyes of all wait upon thee; and thou givest them their meat in due season. 16 Thou openest thine hand, and satisfiest the desire of every living thing. (Psalm 145:15–16)

B. A Story of ______________________

Who is there among you of all his people? his God be with him, and let him go up to Jerusalem, which is in Judah, and build the house of the LORD God of Israel, (he is the God,) which is in Jerusalem. 4 ***And whosoever remaineth in any place where he sojourneth,*** *let the men of his place help him with silver, and with gold, and with goods, and with beasts, beside the freewill offering for the house of God that is in Jerusalem. (Ezra 1:3–4)*

GRACE IN GOD'S REMEMBRANCE

GRACE IN GOD'S PURPOSE

And we know that all things work together for good to them that love God, to them who are the called according to his purpose. (Romans 8:28)

Being justified freely by his grace through the redemption that is in Christ Jesus: (Romans 3:24)

2. HIS ______________________

A. The ______________________ of Israel

For thus saith the LORD, Behold, I will make thee a terror to thyself, and to all thy friends: and they shall fall by the sword of their enemies, and thine eyes shall behold it: and I will give all Judah into the hand of the king of Babylon, and he shall carry them captive into Babylon, and shall slay them with the sword. (Jeremiah 20:4)

And this whole land shall be a desolation, and an astonishment; and these nations shall serve the king of Babylon seventy years. 12 ***And it shall come to pass, when seventy years are accomplished, that I will punish the king of Babylon,*** *and that nation, saith the LORD, for their iniquity, and the land of the Chaldeans, and will make it perpetual desolations. (Jeremiah 25:11–12)*

B. The ______________________ of Israel

Now in Shushan the palace there was a certain Jew, whose name was Mordecai.... 7 And he brought up Hadassah, that is, Esther, his uncle's daughter: for she had neither father nor mother, and the maid was fair and beautiful; whom Mordecai, when her father and mother were dead, took for his own daughter. (Esther 2:5, 7)

Esther had not shewed her people nor her kindred: ***for Mordecai had charged her that she should not shew it.*** *11 And Mordecai walked every day before the court of the women's house, to know how Esther did, and what should become of her. (Esther 2:10–11)*

Go, gather together all the Jews that are present in Shushan, and fast ye for me, and neither eat nor drink three days, night or day: I also and my maidens will fast likewise; and so will I go in unto the king, which is not according to the law: ***and if I perish, I perish.*** *(Esther 4:16)*

3. HIS ______________________

A. For the Children of ______________________

After these things did king Ahasuerus promote Haman the son of Hammedatha the Agagite, and advanced him, and set his seat above all the princes that were with him. 2 And all the king's servants, that were in the king's gate, bowed, and reverenced Haman: for the king had so commanded concerning him. But Mordecai bowed not, nor did him reverence. (Esther 3:1–2)

And Harbonah, one of the chamberlains, said before the king, Behold also, the gallows fifty cubits high, which Haman had made for Mordecai, who had spoken good for the king, standeth in the house of Haman. Then the king said, Hang him thereon. 10 So they hanged Haman on the gallows that he had prepared for Mordecai. Then was the king's wrath pacified. 1 On that day did the king Ahasuerus give the house of Haman the Jews' enemy unto Esther the queen.... 2 And the king took off his ring, which he had taken from Haman, and gave it unto Mordecai....(Esther 7:9–10, 8:1–2)

B. For the Entire ______________________

The Lord is not slack concerning his promise, as some men count slackness; but is longsuffering to us-ward, ***not willing that any should perish,*** *but that all should come to repentance. (2 Peter 3:9)*

Forasmuch as ye know that ye were not redeemed with corruptible things, as silver and gold, from your vain conversation received by tradition from your fathers; 19 But with the precious blood of Christ, as of a lamb without blemish and without spot: (1 Peter 1:18–19)

CONCLUSION

DISCUSSION QUESTIONS

What are some Scripture verses that assure us that God never forgets or forsakes us? What are practical ways we can remind ourselves that God remembers us?

How is chastisement from the Lord evidence of His love? When the Lord does chasten us, how should we respond? (See Proverbs 3:11–12 and Hebrews 12:3–13 for additional study.)

Have you considered how God may want to use you as part of His plan to share His message of salvation with the world? What are opportunities you have available to you now to share the gospel?

NOTES

WEEK ONE | DAY ONE

GOD IS IN CONTROL

Remember the former things of old: for I am God, and there is none else; I am God, and there is none like me, Declaring the end from the beginning, and from ancient times the things that are not yet done, saying, My counsel shall stand, and I will do all my pleasure: Calling a ravenous bird from the east, the man that executeth my counsel from a far country: yea, I have spoken it, I will also bring it to pass; I have purposed it, I will also do it. (Isaiah 46:9–11)

It's easy to look around at our society and see that things are dramatically changing. It is also easy to feel like everything is out of control. Certainly there are many problems around us. There have been repeated economic shocks to our country. The moral underpinnings of our culture have been eroded. Evil and wickedness parade openly in the streets. Places we once thought of as safe, like schools and libraries, have in many cities become platforms for the morally-degrading indoctrination of young people. Yet despite all this, nothing is out of God's control.

Isaiah prophesied to people who were facing an imminent judgment from God that they would see their country defeated in battle, their cities razed to the ground, and even the beautiful Temple that Solomon had built would be demolished. Despite all that impending doom, Isaiah's message was not one of fear. Instead he reminded the people that God was still in control. While that did not mean that things would be easy, or that they would turn out the way people would have preferred, it did mean that there was hope in Him. This is just as true for us today. No matter how wicked our society may become, no matter how much judgment we may rightly receive from the hand of God, no matter how much opposition and even persecution we may face for standing for the truth, God is still in charge.

Today's Growth Principle: Nothing man does can change God's control and ultimate plan for His creation or His people.

REFLECT

What did God say to me as I read today's Scripture and devotion?

____

____

____

____

RESPOND

How does today's Scripture passage apply to my life? What actions can I take because of what I've learned?

____

____

____

____

PRAY

Lord, sometimes as I look around at all the negative changes in my world and in the larger culture, I find it easy to feel afraid. I wonder where it will lead to. Thank You for this reminder today that You are always in control and that You have a good ultimate plan which You will bring about. I pray that You would use me today in Your plan. Help me to point another person to You. Amen.

WEEK ONE | DAY TWO

THE ETERNAL KING

All thy works shall praise thee, O LORD; and thy saints shall bless thee. They shall speak of the glory of thy kingdom, and talk of thy power; To make known to the sons of men his mighty acts, and the glorious majesty of his kingdom. Thy kingdom is an everlasting kingdom, and thy dominion endureth throughout all generations. The LORD upholdeth all that fall, and raiseth up all those that be bowed down. The eyes of all wait upon thee; and thou givest them their meat in due season. (Psalm 145:10–15)

Throughout history, great and powerful empires have risen and fallen. For a time their leaders exercised great authority and power. Then they fell. Some of them left behind impressive ruins that still exist today. Others are little more than a historical curiosity, known only to scholars of antiquity. God gave Nebuchadnezzar a dream that foretold future kingdoms that would follow his empire, until one day God's kingdom would rise—a kingdom that would never fall. "And in the days of these kings shall the God of heaven set up a kingdom, which shall never be destroyed: and the kingdom shall not be left to other people, but it shall break in pieces and consume all these kingdoms, and it shall stand for ever" (Daniel 2:44).

No matter what we see happening around us, God is still the King. He is in charge of individuals and nations, and His purposes cannot be overcome by any power. Though God allows people the freedom to choose to reject Him, even their opposition will in the end be revealed as yet another way for Him to be glorified. "Surely the wrath of man shall praise thee: the remainder of wrath shalt thou restrain" (Psalm 76:10). Martin Luther wrote insightful and comforting words based on this truth:

That word above all earthly powers,
No thanks to them, abideth;
The Spirit and the gifts are ours
Through Him who with us sideth:

Let goods and kindred go,
This mortal life also;
The body they may kill:
God's truth abideth still,
His Kingdom is forever.

Today's Growth Principle: God is in control yesterday, today, and tomorrow; and that will never change.

REFLECT

What did God say to me as I read today's Scripture and devotion?

___

___

___

RESPOND

How does today's Scripture passage apply to my life? What actions can I take because of what I've learned?

___

___

___

PRAY

Lord, I praise You today for Your eternal nature and power. And as I reflect on Your greatness, I'm reminded of how easily I place my confidence or search for security in that which doesn't last. Thank You for this assurance from Your Word today that You uphold those who fall and raise up those who are bowed down. Please uphold me today, and help me to remember all throughout today that You are in control and You are good. Amen.

WEEK ONE | DAY THREE

GOD HAS THE ANSWERS

Then was the secret revealed unto Daniel in a night vision. Then Daniel blessed the God of heaven. Daniel answered and said, Blessed be the name of God for ever and ever: for wisdom and might are his: And he changeth the times and the seasons: he removeth kings, and setteth up kings: he giveth wisdom unto the wise, and knowledge to them that know understanding: (Daniel 2:19–21)

When Nebuchadnezzar asked his wise men to tell them the dream he wanted them to interpret, they could not, because he couldn't remember the dream. He just knew that it was important. He accused them of trying to make something up rather than actually telling him what it meant and ordered all of them to be killed. Daniel asked for time to pray and seek and answer, and God showed him both what Nebuchadnezzar's dream had been and what it meant. Providing that information to the king saved Daniel's life and saw him elevated to a position of power and prominence in Babylon. Daniel did not take credit for that, but instead glorified the God Who has all the answers.

All human knowledge is limited. Even in topics we know a lot about, our perspective is restricted. God knows all the answers to every question we will ever face. He knows what choices we will make, and what the results of those choices will be. He even knows what would have happened if we had chosen something else.

God is in control, and yet He graciously offers to share His guidance and insight with us, if we will simply ask for it in faith. "If any of you lack wisdom, let him ask of God, that giveth to all men liberally, and upbraideth not; and it shall be given him. But let him ask in faith, nothing wavering. For he that wavereth is like a wave of the sea driven with the wind and tossed" (James 1:5–6). In every situation, whether large or small, God has the answers we need.

Today's Growth Principle: God makes His wisdom available for our needs as we ask Him to provide it.

REFLECT

What did God say to me as I read today's Scripture and devotion?

RESPOND

How does today's Scripture passage apply to my life? What actions can I take because of what I've learned?

PRAY

Lord, I need Your wisdom today! And every day! I don't know what today may hold, but I know that I cannot complete the responsibilities You have given to me in a way that honors You without guidance from You. Please give me wisdom for every decision I make and with every person I meet. And please help me to trust in the wisdom You provide and not lean on my own understanding. Amen.

WEEK ONE | DAY FOUR

PERFECT PLANS

As for God, his way is perfect; the word of the LORD is tried: he is a buckler to all them that trust in him. For who is God, save the LORD? and who is a rock, save our God? God is my strength and power: and he maketh my way perfect. He maketh my feet like hinds' feet: and setteth me upon my high places. (2 Samuel 22:31–34)

When she was just six weeks old, Fanny Crosby lost her eyesight because of a doctor's error. Years later she said, "I have heard that this physician never ceased expressing his regret at the occurrence, and that it was one of the sorrows of his life. But if I could meet him now, I would say, 'Thank you, thank you"—over and over again—for making me blind.... Although it may have been a blunder on the physician's part, it was no mistake of God's." In one of her best-known hymns, "All the Way My Savior Leads Me" she wrote:

Heavenly peace, divinest comfort,
Here by faith in Him to dwell
For I know, whate'er befalls me,
Jesus doeth all things well.

We can trust God fully. That does not mean that nothing bad will ever happen to us, but that nothing will deter His plans for us.

David faced many battles in his lifetime. He spent years fleeing from Saul's attempts to kill him. He was betrayed, falsely accused, and had to take his family out of the country for their safety. He knew what it was to be tired and hungry and scared and lonely. Yet despite those difficulties, in 2 Samuel 22:33, David described God's plan for his life and the path He laid for him as "perfect."

The circumstances and sudden changes in our lives never take God by surprise. He never changes His plans. Even before our lives begin, He knows everything about how they will turn out. "Declaring the end from the beginning, and from ancient times the things that are not yet done, saying, My counsel shall stand, and I will do all my pleasure" (Isaiah 46:10).

Today's Growth Principle: The perfection of God's plans for our lives are not measured by our comfort but by His purpose.

REFLECT

What did God say to me as I read today's Scripture and devotion?

____

____

____

RESPOND

How does today's Scripture passage apply to my life? What actions can I take because of what I've learned?

____

____

____

PRAY

Lord, there are many times when the events in my life are out of control. Thank You for the promise of Your Word that You always have a purpose and that You will make even the wrongs of others work for good in my life. Right now, I reaffirm my trust in You. Help me to care more about Your good purposes than my immediate comfort. Please guide my steps in Your perfect way today. Amen.

WEEK ONE | DAY FIVE

GOD NEVER FORGETS

For the earth which drinketh in the rain that cometh oft upon it, and bringeth forth herbs meet for them by whom it is dressed, receiveth blessing from God: But that which beareth thorns and briers is rejected, and is nigh unto cursing; whose end is to be burned. But, beloved, we are persuaded better things of you, and things that accompany salvation, though we thus speak. For God is not unrighteous to forget your work and labour of love, which ye have shewed toward his name, in that ye have ministered to the saints, and do minister. (Hebrews 6:7–10)

There is an old story of a missionary returning from years on the field in Africa by ship. When they arrived in New York City, he saw the huge crowds with banners and marching bands gathered to welcome Teddy Roosevelt who was on the same ship coming home from a safari in Africa. Noticing there was no one to welcome him, the missionary was somewhat discouraged until he was reminded of this truth: *you're not home yet.* There are times when we feel like no one notices or cares what we are doing for God, but even if that is true in this world, it is certain that He is watching. He never misses a thing that we do for Him, and He is righteous to remember it.

When we reach Heaven, we will see that all we did for Christ because of our love for Him, for His glory has been recorded, and we will be rewarded accordingly. These rewards are not for our own glory, but for us to add to our worship and glorifying of Jesus. John saw this in his vision of Heaven, "The four and twenty elders fall down before him that sat on the throne, and worship him that liveth for ever and ever, and cast their crowns before the throne, saying, Thou art worthy, O Lord, to receive glory and honour and power: for thou hast created all things, and for thy pleasure they are and were created" (Revelation 4:10–11).

Today's Growth Principle: We serve a God who is faithful to notice and remember even the smallest things we do in His name.

REFLECT

What did God say to me as I read today's Scripture and devotion?

RESPOND

How does today's Scripture passage apply to my life? What actions can I take because of what I've learned?

PRAY

Lord, You are so good to give me opportunities to serve You and the ability to do so. And then, You even reward me for what You have done through me! Thank You for this assurance from Your Word that even when others do not notice or forget my service to them in Your name, You always see and always will reward me. Please give me opportunities today to serve others for You. Amen.

THAT AT THE NAME OF JESUS EVERY KNEE SHOULD BOW, OF THINGS IN HEAVEN, AND THINGS IN EARTH, AND THINGS UNDER THE EARTH; AND THAT EVERY TONGUE SHOULD CONFESS THAT JESUS CHRIST IS LORD, TO THE GLORY OF GOD THE FATHER.

PHILIPPIANS 2:10–11

WEEK TWO

A KING AND HIS LIMITED POWER

DAY 1: From the Mouth of God

DAY 2: The Bondage of Alcohol

DAY 3: The Danger of Drinking

DAY 4: Do Right on Purpose

DAY 5: Faithful and Diligent

WEEK TWO | STUDY AND DISCUSSION

A KING AND HIS LIMITED POWER

Throughout our lives, leaders in our lives will come and go. And over the years, we'll experience many leaders—especially in political or other secular contexts—who do not love God. While being under ungodly leaders can be discouraging and, at times, frightening, we should remember that our security does not rest in any human. Our security is with the King of kings, who reigns from Heaven. Because of God's sovereignty, all human power is limited. Ahasuerus was an ungodly leader, but God still showed Himself to His people even under the reign of this wicked man.

TEXT

Now it came to pass in the days of Ahasuerus, (this is Ahasuerus which reigned, from
India even unto Ethiopia, over an hundred and seven and twenty provinces:) 2 That in
those days, when the king Ahasuerus sat on the throne of his kingdom, which was in
Shushan the palace, 3 In the third year of his reign, he made a feast unto all his princes
and his servants; the power of Persia and Media, the nobles and princes of the provinces,
being before him: 4 When he shewed the riches of his glorious kingdom and the honor of
his excellent majesty many days, even an hundred and fourscore days. 5 And when these
days were expired, the king made a feast unto all the people that were present in Shushan
the palace, both unto great and small, seven days, in the court of the garden of the king's
palace; 6 Where were white, green, and blue, hangings, fastened with cords of fine linen
and purple to silver rings and pillars of marble: the beds were of gold and silver, upon a
pavement of red, and blue, and white, and black, marble. 7 And they gave them drink in
vessels of gold, (the vessels being diverse one from another,) and royal wine in abundance,
according to the state of the king. 8 And the drinking was according to the law; none did
compel: for so the king had appointed to all the officers of his house, that they should do
according to every man's pleasure. 9 Also Vashti the queen made a feast for the women
in the royal house which belonged to king Ahasuerus. (Esther 1:1–9)

INTRODUCTION

____

____

____

Now in the first year of Cyrus king of Persia, that the word of the LORD spoken by the mouth of Jeremiah might be accomplished, the LORD stirred up the spirit of Cyrus king of Persia, that he made a proclamation throughout all his kingdom, and put it also in writing, saying, 23 Thus saith Cyrus king of Persia, All the kingdoms of the earth hath the LORD God of heaven given me; and he hath charged me to build him an house in Jerusalem, which is in Judah. Who is there among you of all his people? The LORD his God be with him, and let him go up. (2 Chronicles 36:22–23)

1. THE ______________ OF PERSIAN POWER

A. ANALYZED ______________________

B. ANALYZED ______________________

Shown in a Feast

In the third year of his reign, he made a feast unto all his princes and his servants; the power of Persia and Media, the nobles and princes of the provinces, being before him: 4 When he shewed the riches of his glorious kingdom and the honour of his excellent majesty many days, even an hundred and fourscore days. (Esther 1:3–4)

When thou sittest to eat with a ruler, consider diligently what is before thee: 2 and put a knife to thy throat, if thou be a man given to appetite. 3 Be not desirous of his dainties: for they are deceitful meat. (Proverbs 23:1–3)

Shown in Material Possessions

Where were white, green, and blue, hangings, fastened with cords of fine linen and purple to silver rings and pillars of marble: the beds were of gold and silver, upon a pavement of red, and blue, and white, and black, marble. 7 And they gave them drink in vessels of gold, (the vessels being diverse one from another,) and royal wine in abundance, according to the state of the king. (Esther 1:6–7)

C. ANALYZED ______________________

And behold another beast, a second, like to a bear, and it raised up itself on one side, and it had three ribs in the mouth of it between the teeth of it: and they said thus unto it, Arise, devour much flesh. (Daniel 7:5)

D. ANALYZED ______________________

Wherefore God also hath highly exalted him, and given him a name which is above every name: 10 That at the name of Jesus every knee should bow, of things in heaven, and things in earth, and things under the earth; 11 And that every tongue should confess that Jesus Christ is Lord, to the glory of God the Father. (Philippians 2:9–11)

2. THE ______________________ OF A WICKED RULER

On the seventh day, when the heart of the king was merry with wine, he commanded Mehuman, Biztha, Harbona, Bigtha, and Abagtha, Zethar, and Carcas, the seven chamberlains that served in the presence of Ahasuerus the king, 11 To bring Vashti the queen before the king with the crown royal, to shew the people and the princes her beauty: for she was fair to look on. (Esther 1:10–11)

A. AN ILLICIT ____________________

Quote: *"Ahasuerus could not control his passions in regard to women. He had a large harem and kept adding to it."*—**John G. Butler**

Encouraged by Alcohol

He that is slow to anger is better than the mighty; and he that ruleth his spirit than he that taketh a city. (Proverbs 16:32)

He that hath no rule over his own spirit is like a city that is broken down, and without walls. (Proverbs 25:28)

Ye have not eaten bread, neither have ye drunk wine or strong drink: that ye might know that I am the your God. (Deuteronomy 29:6)

And the LORD spake unto Aaron, saying, 9 Do not drink wine nor strong drink, thou, nor thy sons with thee, when ye go into the tabernacle of the congregation, lest ye die: it shall be a statute for ever throughout your generations: (Leviticus 10:8–9)

And the LORD spake unto Moses, saying, 2 Speak unto the children of Israel, and say unto them, When either man or woman shall separate themselves to vow a vow of a Nazarite, to separate themselves unto the LORD: 3 He shall separate himself from wine and strong drink, and shall drink no vinegar of wine, or vinegar of strong drink, neither shall he drink any liquor of grapes, nor eat moist grapes, or dried. 4 All the days of his separation shall he eat nothing that is made of the vine tree, from the kernels even to the husk. (Numbers 6:1–4)

Wine is a mocker, strong drink is raging: and whosoever is deceived thereby is not wise. (Proverbs 20:1)

Quote: *"First the man takes a drink, then the drink takes a drink, and then the drink takes the man."*—**Japanese Proverb**

He that loveth pleasure shall be a poor man: he that loveth wine and oil shall not be rich. (Proverbs 21:17)

ADVANCED BY ANGER

But the queen Vashti refused to come at the king's commandment by his chamberlains: therefore was the king very wroth, and his anger burned in him. (Esther 1:12)

He that is soon angry dealeth foolishly: and a man of wicked devices is hated. (Proverbs 14:17)

For the wrath of man worketh not the righteousness of God. (James 1:20)

B. AN IMMORAL ____________________

There is neither Jew nor Greek, there is neither bond nor free, there is neither male nor female: for ye are all one in Christ Jesus. (Galatians 3:28)

3. THE ____________________ OF UNGODLY MEN

A. THE ____________________ OF QUEEN VASHTI

But the queen Vashti refused to come at the king's commandment by his chamberlains: therefore was the king very wroth, and his anger burned in him. (Esther 1:12)

B. THE ____________________ WITH ADVISORS

Then the king said to the wise men, which knew the times, (for so was the king's manner toward all that knew law and judgment: 14 And the next unto him was Carshena, Shethar, Admatha, Tarshish, Meres, Marsena, and Memucan, the seven princes of Persia and Media, which saw the king's face, and which sat the first in the kingdom;) 15 What shall we do unto the queen Vashti according to law, because she hath not performed the commandment of the king Ahasuerus by the chamberlains? (Esther 1:13–15)

C. THE ____________________ OF THE KING

And the saying pleased the king and the princes; and the king did according to the word of Memucan: 22 For he sent letters into all the king's provinces, into every province according to the writing thereof, and to every people after their language, that every man should bear rule in his own house, and that it should be published according to the language of every people. (Esther 1:21–22)

A Vindictive Command

A Punitive Command

4. THE ____________________ HAND OF GOD

A. THE ____________________ OF MAN

There is a way that seemeth right unto a man, but the end thereof are the ways of death. (Proverbs 16:25)

B. THE ______________________ OF GOD

For my thoughts are not your thoughts, neither are your ways my ways, saith the LORD. *(Isaiah 55:8)*

CONCLUSION

____

____

____

DISCUSSION QUESTIONS

How can Bible prophecy that has already been fulfilled (such as the Persian kingdom replacing the Babylonian kingdom) encourage and reassure us during times of current oppression? What prophecies are we yet waiting to see fulfilled?

____

____

____

What are some of the areas of ungodly reasoning in our world today? In what ways are Christians pressured to comply?

____

____

____

What are some other time periods in history (biblical or later) in which believers may have been tempted to assume God had forsaken them? And how did God work in ways that were not immediately apparent those times?

____

____

____

WEEK TWO | DAY ONE

FROM THE MOUTH OF GOD

For as the heavens are higher than the earth, so are my ways higher than your ways, and my thoughts than your thoughts. For as the rain cometh down, and the snow from heaven, and returneth not thither, but watereth the earth, and maketh it bring forth and bud, that it may give seed to the sower, and bread to the eater: So shall my word be that goeth forth out of my mouth: it shall not return unto me void, but it shall accomplish that which I please, and it shall prosper in the thing whereto I sent it. (Isaiah 55:9–11)

God's Word never fails. Nor does it ever change. The fact that some people refuse to believe what it says or say that it does not make sense does not mean that it is not true. We may struggle to *understand* parts of the Bible, but we should not be reluctant to *believe* that it is true. People don't reject the Bible because there is no evidence it is true. There is much evidence of the reliability of Scripture. They reject it because they do not want to be believe it. J. C. Ryle wrote, "Be very sure of this—people never reject the Bible because they cannot understand it. They understand it too well; they understand that it condemns their own behavior; they understand that it witnesses against their own sins, and summons them to judgment. They try to believe it is false and useless, because they don't like to believe it is true."

The Bible is not a book of ancient history, although all it records is true. The Bible is not a book of religious philosophy, although it spells out the way to God. But the Bible is far more than these. It is the living, active, and powerful Word of God; and it produces results. "For the word of God is quick, and powerful, and sharper than any twoedged sword, piercing even to the dividing asunder of soul and spirit, and of the joints and marrow, and is a discerner of the thoughts and intents of the heart" (Hebrews 4:12). The Bible is God's Word, and everything it says is true and right and unchanging.

Today's Growth Principle: The Bible must be believed and followed, or we are missing the harvest of blessings God has prepared for us.

REFLECT

What did God say to me as I read today's Scripture and devotion?

RESPOND

How does today's Scripture passage apply to my life? What actions can I take because of what I've learned?

PRAY

Lord, I'm so thankful for Your Word and how it pours into my life when I let it. Help me to find practical ways to incorporate more Scripture into my daily walk with You. I believe Your Word wholeheartedly and trust that it will accomplish the things that You said it will. Continue to cultivate that spirit of faith throughout my day. Amen.

WEEK TWO | DAY TWO

THE BONDAGE OF ALCOHOL

Wine is a mocker, strong drink is raging: and whosoever is deceived thereby is not wise. (Proverbs 20:1)

Waylon Prendergast from Tampa, Florida, had been out drinking when he decided to rob a house on his way home. The drunken man forced his way into the house, filled a suitcase he found there with the valuables he discovered, and made his way to the living room. In his stupor he decided it would be a good idea to set a fire to cover his tracks, so he ignited a blaze before making his way out the back door. Thinking he was home free, he continued on to his house—only to find three fire trucks parked outside fighting the blaze he had set to cover his theft from his own home.

According to a study published in The Washington Post, almost one third of adults in America admit they either have now or have had in the past a problem with drinking. The Bible describes alcoholic drinks as being deceitful for a reason. None of those people who now realize they have a problem with it intended to become alcoholics or dependent on their next drink to make it through the day. But that is where the end of the path they set out on leads.

It has become popular in some Christian circles today to downplay the warnings in Scripture regarding alcoholic beverages in the name of Christian liberty and grace. Yet God's grace never leads to bondage. Those who think they are in control of their drinking often take a long time to realize the awful truth. By the time they understand the strength of the chains of addiction that hold them, they are heavily bound. Listening to the voice of wisdom and the warnings from the Word of God guards us from the shame and distress that comes from drinking.

Today's Growth Principle: Just as you would not trust a raging human tempter, refuse to trust the deceitful lures of alcohol.

REFLECT

What did God say to me as I read today's Scripture and devotion?

RESPOND

How does today's Scripture passage apply to my life? What actions can I take because of what I've learned?

PRAY

Lord, thank You for Your warnings concerning the bondage of alcohol. And thank You for the freedom you have given me in Christ to resist temptation. I pray that you would give me the strength to resist bondage in every area of my life so that I may honor You in every area. Thank You for dying on the cross for me so I don't have to live a life of bondage to addiction. Amen.

WEEK TWO | DAY THREE

THE DANGER OF DRINKING

It is not for kings, O Lemuel, it is not for kings to drink wine; nor for princes strong drink: Lest they drink, and forget the law, and pervert the judgment of any of the afflicted. (Proverbs 31:4–5)

There is no question that consuming alcohol affects a person's judgment in a negative way. The National Highway Traffic Safety Administration reports that seventy percent of speeding drivers who have fatal accidents between midnight and 3:00 a.m. are legally drunk. Intoxicated drivers are half as likely to wear seatbelts, and alcohol is involved in more than four out of every five crashes involving drivers who are driving on suspended or revoked licenses or without a license at all.

Alcohol abuse is the fifth leading cause of death in the United States. Nearly half of trauma patients in emergency rooms are there because of alcohol. Those who had been drinking are three times more likely to die in a fire than those who have not. More than one third of adult drownings involve the use of alcohol. Yet people continue to insist that they can "handle it" and know when they have had too much to drink. This is folly because from the first drink alcohol begins to impair judgment.

Every day we are involved in a very real spiritual war. We have a committed enemy who, "as a roaring lion, walketh about, seeking whom he may devour" (1 Peter 5:8). The danger we face day after day requires that we must be diligent and on guard. That is one of the reasons the Bible and especially the book of Proverbs—the book devoted to teaching principles for wise living—contains so many warnings about the dangers of drinking and drunkenness. Alcohol affects our senses, dulls our judgment, and keeps us from fulfilling our duty to God. We should reject it in all of its forms.

Today's Growth Principle: The dangers of spiritual warfare are too great for us to risk allowing our senses and judgment to be dulled by alcoholic drinks.

REFLECT

What did God say to me as I read today's Scripture and devotion?

RESPOND

How does today's Scripture passage apply to my life? What actions can I take because of what I've learned?

PRAY

Lord, help me to always be aware of the consequences of drinking. Help me to think of the people in my life that I would affect with my decision if I were to choose that path. Guide me as I come upon situation in my life that would encourage me to compromise my convictions. Ultimately, Jesus, I don't want to dishonor You in any of my actions. Guide my life in every aspect, I pray. Amen.

WEEK TWO | DAY FOUR

DO RIGHT ON PURPOSE

But Daniel purposed in his heart that he would not defile himself with the portion of the king's meat, nor with the wine which he drank: therefore he requested of the prince of the eunuchs that he might not defile himself. Now God had brought Daniel into favour and tender love with the prince of the eunuchs. And the prince of the eunuchs said unto Daniel, I fear my lord the king, who hath appointed your meat and your drink: for why should he see your faces worse liking than the children which are of your sort? then shall ye make me endanger my head to the king. (Daniel 1:8–10)

One of the unique tools by which the Babylonian Empire was able to control a large expanse of land in the days long before quick communication was to take young men from conquered lands and bring them to Babylon for training. These captives would be brought up and trained in the Babylonian way of doing things. Everything about their past would be changed in an effort to ensure their loyalty would be to Babylon rather than their home countries. Their names, their language, their education, and even their food was changed to get them to conform to the Babylonian system and culture. In most cases, this system worked as designed, but in the case of Daniel, it was met with resistance.

Daniel refused to go along with things that would violate the law of God. He was willing to go to the Babylonian classes. He responded to the name he had been given, Belteshazzar. He was willing to learn and speak the Babylonian language. But he was not willing to eat the food that was provided for him because doing so was contrary to the Old Testament law. Daniel's refusal to eat food from the king's table could have cost him his life. But he was determined to stand for God regardless of the consequences. God intervened to give Daniel favor with those in charge and he was allowed to do right. We should not yield to any pressure to violate God's law regardless of what the consequences may be.

Today's Growth Principle: No one drifts into doing right. It must be chosen on purpose.

REFLECT

What did God say to me as I read today's Scripture and devotion?

RESPOND

How does today's Scripture passage apply to my life? What actions can I take because of what I've learned?

PRAY

God, I want to adopt Daniel's example and be willing to do whatever it takes to stay committed to You. Give me the commitment he demonstrated in the face of bleak circumstances. Help me to make the best out of any trial that tests my faith in You. I trust You in everything and want to commit my day to You no matter what circumstances come about. Thank You for always helping me through hard decisions. Amen.

WEEK TWO | DAY FIVE

FAITHFUL AND DILIGENT

Now in Shushan the palace there was a certain Jew, whose name was Mordecai, the son of Jair, the son of Shimei, the son of Kish, a Benjamite; Who had been carried away from Jerusalem with the captivity which had been carried away with Jeconiah king of Judah, whom Nebuchadnezzar the king of Babylon had carried away. And he brought up Hadassah, that is, Esther, his uncle's daughter: for she had neither father nor mother, and the maid was fair and beautiful; whom Mordecai, when her father and mother were dead, took for his own daughter. (Esther 2:5–7)

Along with thousands of other Jewish people, Mordecai was taken as a captive to Babylon when God sent them out of the land in judgment for their idolatry and disobedience. Far from home as a member of a defeated and despised group of people, Mordecai faced a choice. He could have used what happened to him and his nation as an excuse to turn away from God and live like those around him. Instead, Mordecai determined to maintain his belief in God and his personal integrity. Rather than shirking responsibility, he performed the tasks given to him to the best of his ability. He took care of his younger cousin, Esther, after her parents died. He taught her to believe in the God of Israel, so much so that when her greatest challenge came, she turned to prayer and fasting in response.

Mordecai fulfilled the responsibilities given to him and rose to a position of prominence and influence despite being a foreign captive. He even foiled a plot to kill the king of Persia, uncovering the details in time for the assassins to be stopped.

Mordecai's example assures us that we can do right and do well regardless of our circumstances. No outward condition is an excuse not to do our very best. No difficult circumstance justifies shirking responsibility or doing wrong. We are ultimately working for God, not man and He deserves our best. "Knowing that of the Lord ye shall receive the reward of the inheritance: for ye serve the Lord Christ" (Colossians 3:24).

Today's Growth Principle: If we are diligent no matter what happens, we are prepared for God to use us for His purposes.

REFLECT

What did God say to me as I read today's Scripture and devotion?

____

____

____

RESPOND

How does today's Scripture passage apply to my life? What actions can I take because of what I've learned?

____

____

____

PRAY

Thank You, Lord, for Your faithfulness shown to Your people. It's encouraging to know that the same God who was faithful to Mordecai, is faithful to me. Help me not to take Your faithfulness for granted by not fulfilling the responsibilities You have placed on my life. Give me a vision of what You desire for me to accomplish today. I give this day to You to be obedient to what You have assigned to me. Amen.

FOR PROMOTION COMETH NEITHER FROM THE EAST, NOR FROM THE WEST, NOR FROM THE SOUTH. BUT GOD IS THE JUDGE: HE PUTTETH DOWN ONE, AND SETTETH UP ANOTHER.

PSALM 75:6–7

WEEK THREE

THE UNSEEN DIRECTOR

DAY 1: The Obedience of Jesus

DAY 2: Revealed

DAY 3: Faith and Forgivness

DAY 4: Giving Up on Getting Even

DAY 5: Prepared for God's Use

WEEK THREE | STUDY AND DISCUSSION

THE UNSEEN DIRECTOR

Sometimes when we look around, we doubt God's presence in our lives. But just as the director of a play is there in the background, even if he's unseen by the audience, so our God is always present, even if we can't see exactly what He's doing.

In Esther 2, we see God, the unseen Director of the story, working in each cast member's life to orchestrate events for the good of His people. And we are reminded that just as He had not forgotten the Jews in Shushan, He has not forgotten us.

TEXT

After these things, when the wrath of king Ahasuerus was appeased, he remembered
Vashti, and what she had done, and what was decreed against her. 2 Then said the
king's servants that ministered unto him, Let there be fair young virgins sought for
the king: 3 And let the king appoint officers in all the provinces of his kingdom, that
they may gather together all the fair young virgins unto Shushan the palace, to the
house of the women, unto the custody of Hege the king's chamberlain, keeper of the
women; and let their things for purification be given them: 4 And let the maiden
which pleaseth the king be queen instead of Vashti. And the thing pleased the king;
and he did so. 5 Now in Shushan the palace there was a certain Jew, whose name was
Mordecai, the son of Jair, the son of Shimei, the son of Kish, a Benjamite; 6 Who had
been carried away from Jerusalem with the captivity which had been carried away
with Jeconiah king of Judah, whom Nebuchadnezzar the king of Babylon had carried
away. 7 And he brought up Hadassah, that is, Esther, his uncle's daughter: for she
had neither father nor mother, and the maid was fair and beautiful; whom Mordecai,
when her father and mother were dead, took for his own daughter. 8 So it came to pass,
when the king's commandment and his decree was heard, and when many maidens
were gathered together unto Shushan the palace, to the custody of Hegai, that Esther
was brought also unto the king's house, to the custody of Hegai, keeper of the women. 9
And the maiden pleased him, and she obtained kindness of him; and he speedily gave

her her things for purification, with such things as belonged to her, and seven maidens,
which were meet to be given her, out of the king's house: and he preferred her and her
maids unto the best place of the house of the women. 10 Esther had not shewed her
people nor her kindred: for Mordecai had charged her that she should not shew it. 11
And Mordecai walked every day before the court of the women's house, to know how
Esther did, and what should become of her. 12 Now when every maid's turn was come
to go in to king Ahasuerus, after that she had been twelve months, according to the
manner of the women, (for so were the days of their purifications accomplished, to
wit, six months with oil of myrrh, and six months with sweet odours, and with other
things for the purifying of the women;) 13 Then thus came every maiden unto the king;
whatsoever she desired was given her to go with her out of the house of the women
unto the king's house. 14 In the evening she went, and on the morrow she returned into
the second house of the women, to the custody of Shaashgaz, the king's chamberlain,
which kept the concubines: she came in unto the king no more, except the king
delighted in her, and that she were called by name. 15 Now when the turn of Esther,
the daughter of Abihail the uncle of Mordecai, who had taken her for his daughter,
was come to go in unto the king, she required nothing but what Hegai the king's
chamberlain, the keeper of the women, appointed. And Esther obtained favour in the
sight of all them that looked upon her. 16 So Esther was taken unto king Ahasuerus
into his house royal in the tenth month, which is the month Tebeth, in the seventh year
of his reign. 17 And the king loved Esther above all the women, and she obtained grace
and favour in his sight more than all the virgins; so that he set the royal crown upon
her head, and made her queen instead of Vashti. (Esther 2:1–17)

INTRODUCTION

Quote: *"Fit yourself for God's service; be faithful. He will presently appoint thee. . . . In some unlikely quarter, in a shepherd's hut, or in an artisan's cottage, God has His prepared and appointed instrument. As yet the shaft is hidden in His quiver, in the shadow of His hand; but at the precise moment at which it will tell with the greatest effect, it will be produced and launched on the air."* – **F. B. Meyer**

1. A DEFEATED ____________________

A. A Difficult ________________________

After these things, when the wrath of king Ahasuerus was appeased, he remembered Vashti, and what she had done, and what was decreed against her. (Esther 2:1)

If it please the king, let there go a royal commandment from him, and let it be written among the laws of the Persians and the Medes, that it be not altered, That Vashti come no more before king Ahasuerus; and let the king give her royal estate unto another that is better than she. (Esther 1:19)

He that is slow to wrath is of great understanding: but he that is hasty of spirit exalteth folly. (Proverbs 14:29)

Seest thou a man that is hasty in his words? there is more hope of a fool than of him. (Proverbs 29:20)

B. A Devised _______________

The LORD hath made all things for himself: yea, even the wicked for the day of evil. (Proverbs 16:4)

For the scripture saith unto Pharaoh, Even for this same purpose have I raised thee up, that I might shew my power in thee, and that my name might be declared throughout all the earth. (Romans 9:17)

Then said the king's servants that ministered unto him, Let there be fair young virgins sought for the king. 3 And let the king appoint officers in all the provinces of his kingdom, that they may gather together all the fair young virgins unto Shushan the palace, to the house of the women, unto the custody of Hege the king's chamberlain, keeper of the women; and let their things for purification be given them. (Esther 2:2–3)

And let the maiden which pleaseth the king be queen instead of Vashti. And the thing pleased the king; and he did so. 12 Now when every maid's turn was come to go in to king Ahasuerus, after that she had been twelve months, according to the manner of the women, (for so were the days of their purifications accomplished, to wit, six months with oil of myrrh, and six months with sweet odours, and with other things for the purifying of the women;) (Esther 2:4, 12)

2. A PROMOTED ______________________

Surely the wrath of man shall praise thee: The remainder of wrath shalt thou restrain. (Psalm 76:10)

A. ______________________ in the Palace

Now in Shushan the palace there was a certain Jew, whose name was Mordecai, the son of Jair, the son of Shimei, the son of Kish, a Benjamite; 6 Who had been carried away from Jerusalem with the captivity which had been carried away with Jeconiah king of Judah, whom Nebuchadnezzar the king of Babylon had carried away. (Esther 2:5–6)

B. ______________________ in the Family

And he brought up Hadassah, that is, Esther, his uncle's daughter: for she had neither father nor mother, and the maid was fair and beautiful; whom Mordecai, when her father and mother were dead, took for his own daughter. (Esther 2:7)

For ye have not received the spirit of bondage again to fear; but ye have received the Spirit of adoption, whereby we cry, Abba, Father. 16 The Spirit itself beareth witness with our spirit, that we are the children of God. (Romans 8:15–16)

For promotion cometh neither from the east, nor from the west, nor from the south. 7 But God is the judge: he putteth down one, and setteth up another. (Psalm 75:6–7)

C. ______________________ Brought to the Palace

So it came to pass, when the king's commandment and his decree was heard, and when many maidens were gathered together unto Shushan the palace, to the custody of Hegai, that Esther was brought also unto the king's house, to the custody of Hegai, keeper of the women. (Esther 2:8)

She Was Immediately Favored

And the maiden pleased him, and she obtained kindness of him; and he speedily gave her her things for purification, with such things as belonged to her, and seven maidens, which were meet to be given her, out of the king's house: and he preferred her and her maids unto the best place of the house of the women. (Esther 2:9)

Now God had brought Daniel into favour and tender love with the prince of the eunuchs. (Daniel 1:9)

She Did Not Reveal Her Ancestry

Esther had not shewed her people nor her kindred: for Mordecai had charged her that she should not shew it. (Esther 2:10)

She Waited Twelve Months

Now when every maid's turn was come to go in to king Ahasuerus, after that she had been twelve months, according to the manner of the women, (for so were the days of their purifications accomplished, to wit, six months with oil of myrrh, and six months with sweet odours, and with other things for the purifying of the women;) (Esther 2:12)

Therefore thus will I do unto thee, O Israel: and because I will do this unto thee, prepare to meet thy God, O Israel. (Amos 4:12)

She Was Made the Queen

And the king loved Esther above all the women, and she obtained grace and favour in his sight more than all the virgins; so that he set the royal crown upon her head, and made her queen instead of Vashti. 18 Then the king made a great feast unto all his princes and his servants, even Esther's feast; and he made a release to the provinces, and gave gifts, according to the state of the king. (Esther 2:17–18)

3. A PROMINENT ______________

A. A Plot to ______________________ the King

In those days, while Mordecai sat in the king's gate, two of the king's chamberlains, Bigthan and Teresh, of those which kept the door, were wroth, and sought to lay hands on the king Ahasuerus. And the thing was known to Mordecai… (Esther 2:21–22)

B. The Warning from ____________________

And the thing was known to Mordecai, who told it unto Esther the queen; and Esther certified the king thereof in Mordecai's name. 23 And when inquisition was made of the matter, it was found out; therefore they were both hanged on a tree: and it was written in the book of the chronicles before the king. (Esther 2:22–23)

Love worketh no ill to his neighbour: therefore love is the fulfilling of the law. (Romans 13:10)

Dearly beloved, avenge not yourselves, but rather give place unto wrath: for it is written, Vengeance is mine; I will repay, saith the Lord. (Romans 12:19)

Every man's work shall be made manifest: for the day shall declare it, because it shall be revealed by fire; and the fire shall try every man's work of what sort it is. (1 Corinthians 3:13)

CONCLUSION

For my thoughts are not your thoughts, Neither are your ways my ways, saith the Lord. 9 For as the heavens are higher than the earth, So are my ways higher than your ways, And my thoughts than your thoughts. (Isaiah 55:8–9)

____

____

____

DISCUSSION QUESTIONS

Sometimes we're taken off guard by our anger and not prepared to control it. What are some of the situations in which we might easily be provoked to anger? How can we be prepared in those moments to control our emotions?

Can you look back over your own life and see ways that God used situations that were not part of your plan to bring about a better plan you could not have seen at the time?

In our culture, how do people naturally respond to injustice or personal hurts? How can a strong desire for punishment to come to those who have angered us cause us to lose our joy? How can we acknowledge hurt and hate sin and still find joy in the Lord?

NOTES

WEEK THREE | DAY ONE

THE OBEDIENCE OF JESUS

And being found in fashion as a man, he humbled himself, and became obedient unto death, even the death of the cross. Wherefore God also hath highly exalted him, and given him a name which is above every name: That at the name of Jesus every knee should bow, of things in heaven, and things in earth, and things under the earth; And that every tongue should confess that Jesus Christ is Lord, to the glory of God the Father. (Philippians 2:8–11)

Jesus did not stop being God when He came into the world and was born into a human body. Yet though He was God, even as a baby, He still had to learn to walk and talk and do all the other things that are part of growing to adulthood. The difference between Jesus and everyone else who has ever lived is that He never sinned against God. He was obedient to Mary and Joseph, but most of all He was obedient to His heavenly Father. His will was yielded to God's will, despite what He knew it would require. That was the only way for Him to become the Savior lost mankind needed. "Though he were a Son, yet learned he obedience by the things which he suffered; And being made perfect, he became the author of eternal salvation unto all them that obey him" (Hebrews 5:8–9). As a result of His obedience, Jesus is exalted as Lord of Heaven and Earth.

We sometimes think of being like Jesus in terms of how we deal with others or how we feel about their needs. But in order to be like Him, we must first and foremost be obedient to what God says, no matter what the cost may be. Peter wrote, "For even hereunto were ye called: because Christ also suffered for us, leaving us an example, that ye should follow his steps" (1 Peter 2:21). The sacrificial obedience of Jesus is the model for how we should live each day. This submission to God's will is essential to being like Him.

Today's Growth Principle: Jesus was willing to obey His Father regardless of the consequences, and that is the pattern we must follow.

REFLECT

What did God say to me as I read today's Scripture and devotion?

RESPOND

How does today's Scripture passage apply to my life? What actions can I take because of what I've learned?

PRAY

Lord, I am humbled by Your example of obedience to the Father, "unto death, even the death of the cross." I confess that I am quick to think that I know what is best for my life and even to ask You to bless my plans, rather than submitting to Your plans. I know that You, as the unseen director of my life, have the best plan. I choose today to submit to You and pray that You would help me to walk in submission to You today. Amen.

WEEK THREE | DAY TWO

REVEALED

And the people answered him after this manner, saying, So shall it be done to the man that killeth him. And Eliab his eldest brother heard when he spake unto the men; and Eliab's anger was kindled against David, and he said, Why camest thou down hither? and with whom hast thou left those few sheep in the wilderness? I know thy pride, and the naughtiness of thine heart; for thou art come down that thou mightest see the battle. (1 Samuel 17:27–28)

God does not evaluate people and their fitness for His work based on their outward attributes. What seems to human observers like the perfect person for a job may not measure up to what God knows about how they truly are on the inside. When God sent Samuel to Bethlehem to anoint one of Jesse's sons as the king who would replace Saul, Samuel quickly focused on the oldest. He was the most physically impressive of the group, yet he was not God's choice. "But the LORD said unto Samuel, Look not on his countenance, or on the height of his stature; because I have refused him: for the LORD seeth not as man seeth; for man looketh on the outward appearance, but the LORD looketh on the heart" (1 Samuel 16:7).

We see Eliab's internal failing on display in the story of Goliath. Eliab heard the challenge of the giant, but he did not respond in courage and faith. He was not outraged that this Philistine warrior was blaspheming against the God of Israel. His anger flared instead when his little brother David asked why Goliath was going unchallenged. He falsely accused David of abandoning the family's sheep so he could see the battle and acting in pride.

Eliab's failure was not caused by the threat of Goliath or David's response, but it was revealed in that way. When we face challenges and battles in life, the thing that matters most is not whether we measure up to someone's ideals but whether we are seeking and trusting God from the heart. Others may see our physical attributes or developed skills—or the lack of them, but God sees our heart.

Today's Growth Principle: The heart that is pursuing after and trusting in God will be equipped to face the challenges of life with confidence in God.

REFLECT

What did God say to me as I read today's Scripture and devotion?

____

____

____

____

RESPOND

How does today's Scripture passage apply to my life? What actions can I take because of what I've learned?

____

____

____

____

PRAY

Lord, thank You for Your faithful work in my life that equips me to serve You. Sometimes I find myself comparing myself to others and feeling inadequate. Today, help me respond to You from my heart, trusting You and pursuing a closer relationship with You. Help me to live today with confidence in You. Amen.

WEEK THREE | DAY THREE

FAITH AND FORGIVENESS

And his brethren also went and fell down before his face; and they said, Behold, we be thy servants. And Joseph said unto them, Fear not: for am I in the place of God? But as for you, ye thought evil against me; but God meant it unto good, to bring to pass, as it is this day, to save much people alive. Now therefore fear ye not: I will nourish you, and your little ones. And he comforted them, and spake kindly unto them. (Genesis 50:18–21)

We would understand if Joseph refused to forgive his brothers. They had done him wrong by selling him into years of slavery and imprisonment. They sold him because just killing him would not have made them a profit. But Joseph did forgive his brothers. His choice to forgive is one of the most amazing stories in Scripture.

Even so, years after Joseph and his brothers had reunited, they were still not confident that Joseph was not holding a grudge. After their father Jacob died and they returned from burying him in the Promised Land, they came to Joseph again to ensure they would not be treated as they treated him. At least thirty years had passed since their offense, but they were not sure Joseph was not holding a grudge against them. Again Joseph declared his forgiveness, and promised to care for them and their families through the years ahead.

The reason Joseph was willing to forgive despite all that had been done to him was his recognition of God's control over the events of his life. Both when it happened and years later, Joseph realized God had a purpose in all that had happened. Though he did not fully understand that purpose until many years later, Joseph was always aware that God was at work. He also recognized that it was not his place to get even with his brothers for what they had done. He was willing to trust that God would exact any retribution that was needed, and leave the matter to Him. Joseph's brothers apparently spent years burdened with guilt. But Joseph, with trust in God and His plan, was free through forgiveness.

Today's Growth Principle: Forgiveness requires us to believe that God is in control, and that He will ultimately do what is right.

REFLECT

What did God say to me as I read today's Scripture and devotion?

RESPOND

How does today's Scripture passage apply to my life? What actions can I take because of what I've learned?

PRAY

Father, I easily forget that my willingness to forgive others is an expression of my trust in You. Thank You for the example of Joseph and the freedom he lived in because of his trust in You, even when he was so greatly sinned against. Please show me if there is an area in my life in which I am harboring bitterness, and please give me the grace to forgive as an expression of my faith in You. Amen.

WEEK THREE | DAY FOUR

GIVING UP ON GETTING EVEN

Recompense to no man evil for evil. Provide things honest in the sight of all men. If it be possible, as much as lieth in you, live peaceably with all men. Dearly beloved, avenge not yourselves, but rather give place unto wrath: for it is written, Vengeance is mine; I will repay, saith the Lord. Therefore if thine enemy hunger, feed him; if he thirst, give him drink: for in so doing thou shalt heap coals of fire on his head. Be not overcome of evil, but overcome evil with good. (Romans 12:17–21)

Every one of us knows what it feels like to be mistreated by someone else. Maybe it was a case of our actions being misunderstood or our motives being mischaracterized. Maybe it was being cheated in a financial transaction or being slandered or falsely accused. Whether the offense is small or large, the natural tendency is for us to want to get even. We want the person who has hurt us to experience the pain we feel. We want the person who has caused us grief to know the weight of tears. Although this is a natural reaction, it is not the right reaction. Rather than getting even, we are commanded to leave vengeance in God's hands. He is more than capable of seeing to it that justice is done.

In Peter's description of the suffering of the Lord, he wrote, "Who, when he was reviled, reviled not again; when he suffered, he threatened not; but committed himself to him that judgeth righteously" (1 Peter 2:23). Rather than seeking justice, Jesus instead asked for forgiveness for those who were doing Him wrong. Instead of speaking the word that would have brought legions of angels to His side, He remained silent. Jesus would have been fully justified in unleashing the power of creation on those who mocked Him, beat Him, spit on Him and nailed Him to the cross. But He did not. If Jesus can trust God in such circumstances, we can do the same in the face of far lesser insults and injuries we endure.

Today's Growth Principle: We will never be able to forgive others unless we are willing to trust God to do what is right on our behalf.

REFLECT

What did God say to me as I read today's Scripture and devotion?

RESPOND

How does today's Scripture passage apply to my life? What actions can I take because of what I've learned?

PRAY

Lord, thank You for Your example of enduring evil without retaliating. Sometimes I make so much of the wrongs that are committed against me. But when I remember what was done to You—and all that You suffered to offer me forgiveness—it puts things into perspective. Help me to forgive others with the forgiveness You have given to me. Help me to live today with a spirit that is quick to forgive as a reflection of Your grace in my life. Amen.

WEEK THREE | DAY FIVE

PREPARED FOR GOD'S USE

Listen, O isles, unto me; and hearken, ye people, from far; The LORD hath called me from the womb; from the bowels of my mother hath he made mention of my name. And he hath made my mouth like a sharp sword; in the shadow of his hand hath he hid me, and made me a polished shaft; in his quiver hath he hid me; And said unto me, Thou art my servant, O Israel, in whom I will be glorified. (Isaiah 49:1–3)

God has a purpose and a plan for each of our lives, and He has things He wants us to accomplish for His kingdom. Paul wrote, "For we are his workmanship, created in Christ Jesus unto good works, which God hath before ordained that we should walk in them" (Ephesians 2:10). In order to fulfill our mission, however, we must be prepared for God's use. Soldiers, even in a time of war, are not sent directly into battle, but rather go through training at boot camp. In the same way, we should not expect to immediately or automatically have everything we need for God's work. We need to grow in grace as He prepares and polishes us for His service.

We don't need to be worried about whether what we are doing is public and will be known by others. Instead, we need to trust God to use us in His time in whatever way He chooses. F. B. Meyer wrote, "Fit yourself for God's service; be faithful. He will presently appoint thee. In some unlikely quarter, in a shepherd's hut, or in an artisan's cottage, God has His prepared and appointed instrument. As yet the shaft is hidden in His quiver, in the shadow of His hand; but at the precise moment at which it will tell with the greatest effect, it will be produced and launched on the air." Preparing arrows and polishing the shafts took a great deal of time in Bible days. It was not something done quickly, but once the arrow was prepared, it would fly straight to the target.

Today's Growth Principle: We must never rebel against the timing or the process by which God prepares us for His service.

REFLECT

What did God say to me as I read today's Scripture and devotion?

____

____

____

____

RESPOND

How does today's Scripture passage apply to my life? What actions can I take because of what I've learned?

____

____

____

____

PRAY

Lord, it's incredible to realize that You are not only sovereign over all, but that You have a plan specifically for my life. Forgive me for how quick I am to question Your care and Your timing. Sometimes I think I know best without even recognizing that I'm rebelling against Your plan. I pray that You would help me today to yield to You in all things and that You would give me opportunities today to be used by You. Amen.

AND I WILL BLESS THEM THAT BLESS THEE, AND CURSE HIM THAT CURSETH THEE: AND IN THEE SHALL ALL FAMILIES OF THE EARTH BE BLESSED.

GENESIS 12:3

WEEK FOUR

POWER AND PROVIDENCE

WEEK FOUR | STUDY AND DISCUSSION

POWER AND PROVIDENCE

Fear is one of the most crippling emotions we can experience. Sometimes following the will of God for our lives is terrifying. He may pull us out of our comfort zone and ask us to do something that seems daunting. Esther provides us with an excellent example of someone who obeyed God even though His plan for her was intimidating. Like Esther, you can confidently approach your greatest fears with the knowledge that you serve an all-powerful God who can provide whatever is needed to fulfill His will.

TEXT

After these things did king Ahasuerus promote Haman the son of Hammedatha the
Agagite, and advanced him, and set his seat above all the princes that were with him. 2
And all the king's servants, that were in the king's gate, bowed, and reverenced Haman:
for the king had so commanded concerning him. But Mordecai bowed not, nor did him
reverence. 3 Then the king's servants, which were in the king's gate, said unto Mordecai,
Why transgressest thou the king's commandment? 4 Now it came to pass, when they
spake daily unto him, and he hearkened not unto them, that they told Haman, to see
whether Mordecai's matters would stand: for he had told them that he was a Jew. 5
And when Haman saw that Mordecai bowed not, nor did him reverence, then was
Haman full of wrath. 6 And he thought scorn to lay hands on Mordecai alone; for
they had shewed him the people of Mordecai: wherefore Haman sought to destroy all
the Jews that were throughout the whole kingdom of Ahasuerus, even the people of
Mordecai. 7 In the first month, that is, the month Nisan, in the twelfth year of king
Ahasuerus, they cast Pur, that is, the lot, before Haman from day to day, and from
month to month, to the twelfth month, that is, the month Adar. 8 And Haman said
unto king Ahasuerus, There is a certain people scattered abroad and dispersed among
the people in all the provinces of thy kingdom; and their laws are diverse from all
people; neither keep they the king's laws: therefore it is not for the king's profit to suffer

them. 9 If it please the king, let it be written that they may be destroyed: and I will pay ten thousand talents of silver to the hands of those that have the charge of the business, to bring it into the king's treasuries. 10 And the king took his ring from his hand, and gave it unto Haman the son of Hammedatha the Agagite, the Jews' enemy. 11 And the king said unto Haman, The silver is given to thee, the people also, to do with them as it seemeth good to thee. 12 Then were the king's scribes called on the thirteenth day of the first month, and there was written according to all that Haman had commanded unto the king's lieutenants, and to the governors that were over every province, and to the rulers of every people of every province according to the writing thereof, and to every people after their language; in the name of king Ahasuerus was it written, and sealed with the king's ring. (Esther 3:1–12)

INTRODUCTION

____

____

____

1. A ______________________ FOR POWER

A. ______________________ Is Promoted

After these things did king Ahasuerus promote Haman the son of Hammedatha the Agagite, and advanced him, and set his seat above all the princes that were with him. 2 And all the king's servants, that were in the king's gate, bowed, and reverenced Haman: for the king had so commanded concerning him. But Mordecai bowed not, nor did him reverence. (Esther 3:1–2)

HIS ANCESTRY

HIS ADVANCEMENT

And the beast which I saw was like unto a leopard, and his feet were as the feet of a bear, and his mouth as the mouth of a lion: ***and the dragon gave him his power, and his seat, and great authority.*** *6 And he opened his mouth in blasphemy against God, to blaspheme his name, and his tabernacle, and them* *that dwell in heaven. 7* ***And it was given unto him to make war with the saints, and to overcome them:*** *and power was given him over all kindreds, and tongues, and nations. 8 And all that dwell upon the earth shall worship him, whose names are not written in the book of life of the Lamb slain from the foundation of the world. (Revelation 13:2, 6–8)*

B. ______________________________ Refuses to Bow

. . .But Mordecai bowed not, nor did him reverence. 3 Then the king's servants, which were in the king's gate, said unto Mordecai, Why transgressest thou the king's commandment? 4 Now it came to pass, when they spake daily unto him, and he hearkened not unto them, that they told Haman, to see whether Mordecai's matters would stand: for he had told them that he was a Jew. (Esther 3:2–4)

MORDECAI'S DISOBEDIENCE

Thou shalt not bow down thyself to them, nor serve them: for I the Lord thy God am a jealous God, visiting the iniquity of the fathers upon the children unto the third and fourth generation of them that hate me. (Exodus 20:5)

Quote: *"Mordecai's controversy with Haman was not a personal quarrel with a proud and difficult man. It was Mordecai's declaration that he was on God's side in the national struggle between the Jews and the Amalekites."*
—Warren Wiersbe

MORDECAI'S DECLARATION

Then the king's servants, which were in the king's gate, said unto Mordecai, Why transgressest thou the king's commandment? 4 Now it came to pass, when they spake daily unto him, and he hearkened not unto them, that they told Haman, to see whether Mordecai's matters would stand: for he had told them that he was a Jew. (Esther 3:3–4)

2. THE ____________________ OF HAMAN

And when Haman saw that Mordecai bowed not, nor did him reverence, then was Haman full of wrath. 6 And he thought scorn to lay hands on Mordecai alone; for they had shewed him the people of Mordecai: wherefore Haman sought to destroy all the Jews that were throughout the whole kingdom of Ahasuerus, even the people of Mordecai. (Esther 3:5–6)

Quote: *"Haman's hatred for Mordecai soon developed into hatred for the whole Jewish race. Haman could have reported Mordecai's crimes to the king, and the king would have imprisoned Mordecai or perhaps had him executed, but that would not have satisfied Haman's lust for revenge."*—**Warren Wiersbe**

A. Haman's ___________________________

In the first month, that is, the month Nisan, in the twelfth year of king Ahasuerus, they cast Pur, that is, the lot, before Haman from day to day, and from month to month, to the twelfth month, that is, the month Adar. (Esther 3:7)

And Aaron shall cast lots upon the two goats; one lot for the Lord, and the other lot for the scapegoat. (Leviticus 16:8)

And Haman said unto king Ahasuerus, There is a certain people scattered abroad and dispersed among the people in all the provinces of thy kingdom; and their laws are diverse from all people; neither keep they the king's laws: therefore it is not for the king's profit to suffer them. (Esther 3:8)

If it please the king, let it be written that they may be destroyed: and I will pay ten thousand talents of silver to the hands of those that have the charge of the business, to bring it into the king's treasuries. (Esther 3:9)

Quote: *"Scholars estimate this amount of silver as being close to four billion dollars in our money. It was 375 tons of silver. Herodotus, an ancient historian, said that this amount of money was two-thirds of the entire revenue of the Persian government."*—**John G. Butler**

B. The King's ___________________________

And the king took his ring from his hand, and gave it unto Haman the son of Hammedatha the Agagite, the Jews' enemy. 11 And the king said unto Haman, The silver is given to thee, the people also, to do with them as it seemeth good to thee. (Esther 3:10–11)

Then they came near, and spake before the king concerning the king's decree; Hast thou not signed a decree, that every man that shall ask a petition of any God or man within thirty days, save of thee, O king, shall be cast into the den of lions? The king answered and said, The thing is true, according to the law of the Medes and Persians, which altereth not. (Daniel 6:12)

And I will bless them that bless thee, and curse him that curseth thee: and in thee shall all families of the earth be blessed. (Genesis 12:3)

Then were the king's scribes called on the thirteenth day of the first month, and there was written according to all that Haman had commanded unto the king's lieutenants, and to the governors that were over every province, and to the rulers of every people of every province according to the writing thereof, and to every people after their language; in the name of king Ahasuerus was it written, and sealed with the king's ring. 13 And the letters were sent by posts into all the king's provinces, to destroy, to kill, and to cause to perish, all Jews, both young and old, little children and women, in one day, even upon the thirteenth day of the twelfth month, which is the month Adar, and to take the spoil of them for a prey. 14 The copy of the writing for a commandment to be given in every province was published unto all people, that they should be ready against that day. (Esther 3:12–14)

C. The City's ______________________________

The posts went out, being hastened by the king's commandment, and the decree was given in Shushan the palace. And the king and Haman sat down to drink; but the city Shushan was perplexed. (Esther 3:15)

When the righteous are in authority, the people rejoice: but when the wicked beareth rule, the people mourn. (Proverbs 29:2)

When the wicked rise, men hide themselves: but when they perish, the righteous increase. (Proverbs 28:28)

Quote: *"While the king and Haman drank, the city was distressed. After all, if one race of people can be wiped out by a decree of the king, what about other races? Governments that are evil do not produce tranquility to their people, rather they produce troubling hearts and minds."*—**John G. Butler**

3. A ________________ FOR SALVATION

A. Mordecai's ________________

Mordecai's Mourning

When Mordecai perceived all that was done, Mordecai rent his clothes, and put on sackcloth with ashes, and went out into the midst of the city, and cried with a loud and a bitter cry; 2 And came even before the king's gate: for none might enter into the king's gate clothed with sackcloth. (Esther 4:1–2)

The Jews of the Empire Mourning

And in every province, whithersoever the king's commandment and his decree came, there was great mourning among the Jews, and fasting, and weeping, and wailing; and many lay in sackcloth and ashes. (Esther 4:3)

Mordecai's Communication

So Esther's maids and her chamberlains came and told it her. Then was the queen exceedingly grieved; and she sent raiment to clothe Mordecai, and to take away his sackcloth from him: but he received it not. 5 Then called Esther for Hatach, one of the king's chamberlains, whom he had appointed to attend upon her, and gave him a commandment to Mordecai, to know what it was, and why it was. (Esther 4:4–5)

Mordecai's Reply

So Hatach went forth to Mordecai unto the street of the city, which was before the king's gate. 7 And Mordecai told him of all that had happened unto him, and of the sum of the money that Haman had promised to pay to the king's treasuries for the Jews, to destroy them. 8 Also he gave him the copy of the writing of the decree that was given at Shushan to destroy them, to shew it unto Esther, and to declare it unto her, and to charge her that she should go in unto the king, to make supplication unto him, and to make request before him for her people. 9 And Hatach came and told Esther the words of Mordecai. (Esther 4:6–9)

Again Esther spake unto Hatach, and gave him commandment unto Mordecai; 11 All the king's servants, and the people of the king's provinces, do know, that whosoever, whether man or women, shall come unto the king into the inner court, who is not called, there is one law of his to put him to death, except such to whom the king shall hold out the golden sceptre, that he may live: but I have not been called to come in unto the king these thirty days. 12 And they told to Mordecai Esther's words. (Esther 4:10–12)

B. Mordecai's ______________________________

Then Mordecai commanded to answer Esther, Think not with thyself that thou shalt escape in the king's house, more than all the Jews. 14 For if thou altogether holdest thy peace at this time, then shall there enlargement and deliverance arise to the Jews from another place; but thou and thy father's house shall be destroyed: and who knoweth whether thou art come to the kingdom for such a time as this? (Esther 4:13–14)

C. Esther's __________________

Faith to Fast

Faith to Die

Then Esther bade them return Mordecai this answer, 16 Go, gather together all the Jews that are present in Shushan, and fast ye for me, and neither eat nor drink three days, night or day: I also and my maidens will fast likewise; and so will I go in unto the king, which is not according to the law: and if I perish, I perish. 17 So Mordecai went his way, and did according to all that Esther had commanded him. (Esther 4:15–17)

CONCLUSION

Therefore we are always confident, knowing that, whilst we are at home in the body, we are absent from the Lord: 7 (For we walk by faith, not by sight:) 8 We are confident, I say, and willing rather to be absent from the body, and to be present with the Lord. (2 Corinthians 5:6–8)

The preparations of the heart in man, and the answer of the tongue, is from the Lord. 2 All the ways of a man are clean in his own eyes; but the Lord weigheth the spirits. 3 Commit thy works unto the Lord, and thy thoughts shall be established. (Proverbs 16:1–3)

DISCUSSION QUESTIONS

In what ways are Christians today pressured to bow to the world to avoid conflict or to avoid being "canceled"?

What are some Bible promises that can help us trust that "God's got this" when we receive devastating or frightening news? How can we remind ourselves of these promises when we feel desperate?

Romans 12:15 says, "Rejoice with them that do rejoice, and weep with them that weep." Sometimes, however, we find it hard to mourn with people, preferring instead to try to cheer them up. What are ways we can share in other's grief while still helping them trust in God? What are some helpful and unhelpful responses toward those who are grieving?

WEEK FOUR | DAY ONE

"IF I PERISH"

Then Esther bade them return Mordecai this answer, Go, gather together all the Jews that are present in Shushan, and fast ye for me, and neither eat nor drink three days, night or day: I also and my maidens will fast likewise; and so will I go in unto the king, which is not according to the law: and if I perish, I perish. So Mordecai went his way, and did according to all that Esther had commanded him. (Esther 4:15–17)

When Mordecai learned of Haman's plan to have all the Jews in the Persian empire killed, he sent word to Esther to go and talk to the king and plead the cause of her people. Under the custom of the time, entering the king's presence without an invitation carried a death sentence unless he extended his scepter to grant permission. This practice was probably at least in part a guard against an assassination attempt, ensuring that only those the king knew and trusted would be able to get close to him. But it also shows us something of King Ahasuerus' maniacal ego.

Esther recognized the danger involved in what she was about to do. But she also recognized the importance of her mission. Rather than fearing the risk, she prayed and fasted, and determined to approach the king to plead the lives of the Jewish people—even if it cost her own life.

Thankfully most of us are not faced with literal life or death consequences when we are called to take a stand for Christ. While we like to think we would make the right choice in such a situation, that is not guaranteed. When Jesus warned Peter that he would deny Him, Peter completely rejected the idea. "But he spake the more vehemently, If I should die with thee, I will not deny thee in any wise. Likewise also said they all" (Mark 14:31). Yet when he was pointed out as a follower of Jesus, Peter swore an oath that he didn't even know the Lord.

When we are faced with speaking up for God or keeping silent, we must trust God enough to obey Him, no matter what the consequences of that choice will be.

Today's Growth Principle: We should be faithful to Christ in everything both large and small, regardless of the cost.

REFLECT

What did God say to me as I read today's Scripture and devotion?

RESPOND

How does today's Scripture passage apply to my life? What actions can I take because of what I've learned?

PRAY

Lord, I acknowledge my weakness in standing up for You. I pray that today You would give me the strength to speak boldly for You and to proclaim Your name. I pray that you would give me an opportunity today to speak of You to others and to point them to You. Amen.

WEEK FOUR | DAY TWO

CONSISTENCY

All the presidents of the kingdom, the governors, and the princes, the counsellors, and the captains, have consulted together to establish a royal statute, and to make a firm decree, that whosoever shall ask a petition of any God or man for thirty days, save of thee, O king, he shall be cast into the den of lions. Now, O king, establish the decree, and sign the writing, that it be not changed, according to the law of the Medes and Persians, which altereth not. Wherefore king Darius signed the writing and the decree. (Daniel 6:7–9)

Most ancient kingdoms that were ruled by a monarch were at the whim of whoever held the highest office. What was a hard and fast rule yesterday could be completely different by tomorrow if the king changed his mind. One of the notable exceptions to this trend was the empire of the Medes and Persians. Recognizing the importance of stability and certainty to the people of their kingdoms, they refused to allow even the king to alter a decree once it had been approved and signed. This meant that everyone could know in advance exactly what they could or could not do and what the consequences would be.

There is enormous value in dependability, not just in government, but in our personal lives as well. Character is revealed in consistency. F. B. Meyer wrote, "The supreme test of goodness is not in the greater but in the smaller incidents of our character and practice; not what we are when standing in the searchlight of public scrutiny, but when we reach the firelight flicker of our homes; not what we are when some clarion-call rings through the air, summoning us to fight for life and liberty, but our attitude when we are called to sentry-duty in the gray morning, when the watch-fire is burning low. It is impossible to be our best at the supreme moment if character is corroded and eaten into by daily inconsistency, unfaithfulness, and besetting sin."

Today's Growth Principle: Being consistent and dependable is vital to being effective in our work for God.

REFLECT

What did God say to me as I read today's Scripture and devotion?

RESPOND

How does today's Scripture passage apply to my life? What actions can I take because of what I've learned?

PRAY

Father, I'm thankful for Your unchanging character and Your great faithfulness in my life. Thank You for Your promise in James 1:17 that You are the "Father of lights, with whom is no variableness, neither shadow of turning." In contrast, I am often so fickle and easily swayed by adversity or my changing circumstances. Help me to live today with the dependability that would point others to You. Help me to reflect Your character in this way so that I can ultimately reflect You to this world. Amen.

WEEK FOUR | DAY THREE

THE DANGERS OF PRIDE

And all the king's servants, that were in the king's gate, bowed, and reverenced Haman: for the king had so commanded concerning him. But Mordecai bowed not, nor did him reverence. Then the king's servants, which were in the king's gate, said unto Mordecai, Why transgressest thou the king's commandment? Now it came to pass, when they spake daily unto him, and he hearkened not unto them, that they told Haman, to see whether Mordecai's matters would stand: for he had told them that he was a Jew. And when Haman saw that Mordecai bowed not, nor did him reverence, then was Haman full of wrath. (Esther 3:2–5)

Haman was a wicked man, but he knew how to manipulate the systems of the Persian empire. Using the tools of flattery, bribery, and corruption, he rose to a prominent position and gained favor with the ruler—so much so that the king commanded the servants in the palace to bow to him just as they would have done for the king. Yet despite that promotion, Haman was not content. There was one man, Mordecai, who refused to bow before him.

As a Jew, Mordecai was committed to the worship of the God of Israel alone. So even though everyone else in the palace bowed before him, Haman was enraged because there was one person who would not. His rage led him to plot the extermination of all the Jewish people, which eventually led to his own downfall.

Pride is such an ugly sin. But it's easier to see in others than it is in ourselves. Yet, pride keeps us from God. James 4:6 tells us, "But he giveth more grace. Wherefore he saith, God resisteth the proud, but giveth grace unto the humble."

Pride also brings contention to our relationships. "Only by pride cometh contention: but with the well advised is wisdom" (Proverbs 13:10). Haman's pride created contention between him and Mordecai. If we want thriving relationships with others, we should be willing to humble ourselves: "Likewise, ye younger, submit yourselves unto the elder. Yea, all of you be subject one to another, and be clothed with humility: for God resisteth the proud, and giveth grace to the humble" (1 Peter 5:5).

Today's Growth Principle: Ask the Lord to show you any pride in your life that you do not see, and receive His grace to turn from it.

REFLECT

What did God say to me as I read today's Scripture and devotion?

RESPOND

How does today's Scripture passage apply to my life? What actions can I take because of what I've learned?

PRAY

God, please reveal to me any amount of pride in my life that I cannot see. I don't want to be so consumed with it that I don't even recognize it. I ask for Your cleansing from any pride that has wedged its way into my heart. Help me to consistently understand how pride effects my relationships with others and how it can hinder my relationship with You. Thank You for Your example of humility toward me. Amen.

WEEK FOUR | DAY FOUR

TRUSTING GOD IN FAMINE

And Elijah the Tishbite, who was of the inhabitants of Gilead, said unto Ahab, As the LORD God of Israel liveth, before whom I stand, there shall not be dew nor rain these years, but according to my word. And the word of the LORD came unto him, saying, Get thee hence, and turn thee eastward, and hide thyself by the brook Cherith, that is before Jordan. And it shall be, that thou shalt drink of the brook; and I have commanded the ravens to feed thee there. (1 Kings 17:1–4)

As judgment for the idolatry of His people under the wicked reign of Ahab and Jezebel, God sent Elijah to declare that there would be a drought in the land. In an agricultural economy that was a devastating blow. Knowing how Ahab would respond, God instructed the prophet to hide himself in a spot by a little brook called Cherith, and He promised that He would care for Elijah. While Elijah was not miraculously taken out of the land and away from the drought and famine, He was fed by ravens that God sent and could drink the water from the brook. When the brook dried up, God sent him to a widow in Jezebel's home country where he stayed until the time of judgment was ended. Again God provided as the little bit of meal and oil that the widow had lasted until the famine was over.

God does not promise us that we will not experience the hardships that occur where we live, whether those are the result of divine judgment or from a natural disaster. While God could and sometimes does directly deliver His people from such events, most of the time He simply provides for them during the time of hardship.

Sometimes, God's provision is not done in the way we might have envisioned. Taking food from an unclean bird like a raven was probably not what Elijah would have chosen. But it was the way God ordained his deliverance, and Elijah trusted and obeyed God regardless of his circumstances. And he was privileged to experience the miraculous provision of God.

Today's Growth Principle: Having faith in God's provision and protection requires allowing Him to work in whatever way He chooses to accomplish His purpose.

REFLECT

What did God say to me as I read today's Scripture and devotion?

RESPOND

How does today's Scripture passage apply to my life? What actions can I take because of what I've learned?

PRAY

Lord, thank You for providing for me in times of uncertainty. Even though I don't always understand Your way of accomplishing Your will in my life, I will choose to trust You today. Thank You for those hard times because they merely draw me closer to You and Your Word. Give me a fresh perspective of the trials ahead and help me to see the purposes You are working out for my good. Amen.

WEEK FOUR | DAY FIVE

THE WINNING SIDE

And he opened his mouth in blasphemy against God, to blaspheme his name, and his tabernacle, and them that dwell in heaven. And it was given unto him to make war with the saints, and to overcome them: and power was given him over all kindreds, and tongues, and nations. And all that dwell upon the earth shall worship him, whose names are not written in the book of life of the Lamb slain from the foundation of the world. (Revelation 13:6–8)

The picture that God's Word gives us of the future of our world is not pleasant. We do not know when the events foretold by the prophets and apostles will take place, but they are certain. When the Tribulation comes and evil is given free reign over this world, there will be sorrow and suffering like nothing seen before in all of human history. When the restraining influence of the Holy Spirit is removed, great evil and wickedness will follow. "For the mystery of iniquity doth already work: only he who now letteth will let, until he be taken out of the way" (2 Thessalonians 2:7). This evil will not be rejected by the lost, but instead will be welcomed with open arms and even worshiped.

Though the full measure of this evil will not be revealed until the Tribulation, we see it already working in our world. This is not something new—it was already present in the first century. John wrote, "Little children, it is the last time: and as ye have heard that antichrist shall come, even now are there many antichrists; whereby we know that it is the last time" (1 John 2:18).

This knowledge of the reality of evil and its future spread is not meant to discourage us. It is a warning we must take seriously, but it does not mean we are doomed to defeat. We are on the winning side. "And they overcame him by the blood of the Lamb, and by the word of their testimony; and they loved not their lives unto the death" (Revelation 12:11).

Today's Growth Principle: Though evil is powerful, it is no match for God's power in the lives of His people.

REFLECT

What did God say to me as I read today's Scripture and devotion?

____

____

____

____

RESPOND

How does today's Scripture passage apply to my life? What actions can I take because of what I've learned?

____

____

____

____

PRAY

God, You are all-powerful, and nothing can overcome You since You have overcome the world. Help me to be discerning of evil that I would not be deceived by it. But also help me to not get discouraged by its spread. Help me to praise You today, even through the spiritual darkness of our world. Please display Your power through my life that others would be pointed to You. Amen.

THE KING'S HEART IS IN THE HAND OF THE LORD, AS THE RIVERS OF WATER: HE TURNETH IT WHITHERSOEVER HE WILL.

PROVERBS 21:1

WEEK FIVE

THE FAVOR OF GOD

DAY 1: Rewarded

DAY 2: Walking by Faith

DAY 3: Prayer and Fasting

DAY 4: Pray First

DAY 5: The Foundation of Prayer

WEEK FIVE | STUDY AND DISCUSSION

THE FAVOR OF GOD

Big life steps can give us extreme anxiety. When facing a difficult situation, we are met with a plethora of unknowns. Terror strikes us as we think about how we will be perceived by others. Fortunately, God invites us to seek Him, the God who has the ability to grant us favor with anyone. He sees us where we are, and He is willing to direct our paths..

TEXT

Now it came to pass on the third day, that Esther put on her royal apparel, and stood in the inner court of the king's house, over against the king's house: and the king sat upon his royal throne in the royal house, over against the gate of the house. 2 And it was so, when the king saw Esther the queen standing in the court, that she obtained favour in his sight: and the king held out to Esther the golden sceptre that was in his hand. So Esther drew near, and touched the top of the sceptre. 3 Then said the king unto her, What wilt thou, queen Esther? and what is thy request? it shall be even given thee to the half of the kingdom. 4 And Esther answered, If it seem good unto the king, let the king and Haman come this day unto the banquet that I have prepared for him. 5 Then the king said, Cause Haman to make haste, that he may do as Esther hath said. So the king and Haman came to the banquet that Esther had prepared. 6 And the king said unto Esther at the banquet of wine, What is thy petition? and it shall be granted thee: and what is thy request? even to the half of the kingdom it shall be performed. 7 Then answered Esther, and said, My petition and my request is; 8 If I have found favour in the sight of the king, and if it please the king to grant my petition, and to perform my request, let the king and Haman come to the banquet that I shall prepare for them, and I will do to morrow as the king hath said. 9 Then went Haman forth that day joyful and with a glad heart: but when Haman saw Mordecai in the king's gate, that he stood not up, nor moved for him, he was full of indignation against Mordecai. 10 Nevertheless Haman refrained himself: and when he came home, he sent and called for his friends, and Zeresh his wife. 11 And Haman told them of the glory of his riches, and the multitude of his children, and all the things wherein the king had promoted him, and how he had advanced him above the princes and servants of the king. 12 Haman said moreover, Yea, Esther the queen did let no man come in with the king unto the banquet that she had prepared but myself; and to morrow am I invited unto her also with the king. (Esther 5:1–12)

INTRODUCTION

____

____

____

And in every province, whithersoever the king's commandment and his decree came, there was great mourning among the Jews, and fasting, and weeping, and wailing; and many lay in sackcloth and ashes. (Esther 4:3)

...And who knoweth whether thou art come to the kingdom for such a time as this? (Esther 4:14)

1. ESTHER'S ____________________ OF THE KING

The king's heart is in the hand of the LORD, as the rivers of water: he turneth it whithersoever he will. (Proverbs 21:1)

A. ____________________

Go, gather together all the Jews that are present in Shushan, and fast ye for me, and neither eat nor drink three days, night or day: I also and my maidens will fast likewise; and so will I go in unto the king, which is not according to the law: and if I perish, I perish. 17 So Mordecai went his way, and did according to all that Esther had commanded him. (Esther 4:16–17)

The preparations of the heart in man, and the answer of the tongue, is from the LORD. *3 Commit thy works unto the* LORD, *and thy thoughts shall be established. (Proverbs 16:1, 3)*

Then Daniel went to his house, and made the thing known to Hananiah, Mishael,
and Azariah, his companions: 18 That they would desire mercies of the God of
heaven concerning this secret; that Daniel and his fellows should not perish with
the rest of the wise men of Babylon. 19 Then was the secret revealed unto Daniel
in a night vision. Then Daniel blessed the God of heaven. 20 Daniel answered
and said, Blessed be the name of God for ever and ever: for wisdom and might
are his: 21 And he changeth the times and the seasons: he removeth kings, and
setteth up kings: he giveth wisdom unto the wise, and knowledge to them that
know understanding. (Daniel 2:17–21)

Quote: *"Some people think God does not like to be troubled with our constant coming and asking. The way to trouble God is not to come at all."*—**D. L. Moody**

Quote: *"If Christians spent as much time praying as grumbling, they would soon have nothing to grumble about."*—**Author unknown**

B. ______________________________

A ROYAL DRESS

Now it came to pass on the third day, that Esther put on her royal apparel…(Esther 5:1)

Quote: *"Esther was concerned whether the king would acknowledge her presence and grant her an audience. If he didn't it could mean her immediate execution, and she knew how unpredictable were his moods."*—**Warren Wiersbe**

Quote: *"Esther prepared herself to meet the king. . . . If you knew you were going to meet the president of the United States at the White House… you would prepare for the meeting."*—**Warren Wiersbe**

A CALM DEMEANOR

…and stood in the inner court of the king's house, over against the king's house. (Esther 5:1)

4 REASONS ESTHER COULD BE CALM IN THE FACE OF DANGER

- The Jews had been fasting and praying for three days, asking God to intervene and save them from annihilation.
- Esther knew that God had covenanted with the Jews to deal with their enemies (Genesis 12:1–3).
- Esther knew that the God of Israel was a forgiving God who would hear His people when they humbled themselves and prayed (2 Chronicles 7:14).
- Esther saw God's favor in that He had already allowed a remnant of Jews to return to their land and rebuild the temple.

Be careful for nothing; but in every thing by prayer and supplication with thanksgiving let your requests be made known unto God. 7 And the peace of God, which passeth all understanding, shall keep your hearts and minds through Christ Jesus. (Philippians 4:6–7)

Quote: *"One of the greatest needs in the church today is for intercessors who will pray faithfully for a lost world and for a church that desperately needs revival."* **—Warren Wiersbe**

C. ______________________________

And it was so, when the king saw Esther the queen standing in the court, that she obtained favour in his sight… (Esther 5:2)

The king's heart is in the hand of the Lord, as the rivers of water: he turneth it whithersoever he will. (Proverbs 21:1)

…and the king held out to Esther the golden sceptre that was in his hand. So Esther drew near, and touched the top of the sceptre. 3 Then said the king unto her, What wilt thou, queen Esther? and what is thy request? it shall be even given thee to the half of the kingdom. (Esther 5:2–3)

2. ESTHER'S ________________ REGARDING HAMAN

A. Esther Requests ________________________ to a Banquet

And Esther answered, If it seem good unto the king, let the king and Haman come this day unto the banquet that I have prepared for him. (Esther 5:4)

B. Esther Requests a ___________________________ Banquet

*Then the king said, Cause Haman to make haste, that he may do as Esther hath
said. So the king and Haman came to the banquet that Esther had prepared. 6
And the king said unto Esther at the banquet of wine, What is thy petition? and
it shall be granted thee: and what is thy request? even to the half of the kingdom
it shall be performed. 7 Then answered Esther, and said, My petition and my
request is; 8 If I have found favour in the sight of the king, and if it please the king
to grant my petition, and to perform my request, let the king and Haman come
to the banquet that I shall prepare for them, and I will do to morrow as the king
hath said. (Esther 5:5–8)*

C. Haman's _________________________ Increases

Quote: *"What an honor for Haman to attend a special banquet with the king and queen alone and in the queen's private apartment at that! It's unlikely that any official in the empire had ever been so honored. As Haman ate and drank with Ahasuerus and Esther, his confidence grew."*—**Warren Wiersbe**

He Hated Mordecai

Then went Haman forth that day joyful and with a glad heart: but when Haman saw Mordecai in the king's gate, that he stood not up, nor moved for him, he was full of indignation against Mordecai. (Esther 5:9)

He Brags to Friends

*Nevertheless Haman refrained himself: and when he came home, he sent and
called for his friends, and Zeresh his wife. 11 And Haman told them of the glory
of his riches, and the multitude of his children, and all the things wherein the
king had promoted him, and how he had advanced him above the princes and
servants of the king. 12 Haman said moreover, Yea, Esther the queen did let no*

man come in with the king unto the banquet that she had prepared but myself; and to morrow am I invited unto her also with the king. (Esther 5:10–12)

*These six things doth the Lord hate: Yea, seven are an abomination unto him: 17
A proud look, a lying tongue, And hands that shed innocent blood,18 An heart
that deviseth wicked imaginations, Feet that be swift in running to mischief, 19
A false witness that speaketh lies, And he that soweth discord among brethren.
(Proverbs 6:16–19)*

Quote: *"Pride is the ground in which all the other sins grow, and the parent from which all the other sins come."*—**William Barclay**

He Plans to Kill Mordecai

*Yet all this availeth me nothing, so long as I see Mordecai the Jew sitting at the
king's gate. 14 Then said Zeresh his wife and all his friends unto him, Let a
gallows be made of fifty cubits high, and to morrow speak thou unto the king that Mordecai may be hanged thereon: then go thou in merrily with the king unto the banquet. And the thing pleased Haman; and he caused the gallows to be made. (Esther 5:13–14)*

Quote: *"Not one to waste time, Haman ordered that the gallows be made. We're not sure whether the gallows itself was seventy-five feet high or whether it was put in a prominent place that lifted it to that height, such as the city wall or the roof of a building."*—**Warren Wiersbe**

He that is slow to wrath is of great understanding: but he that is hasty of spirit exalteth folly. (Proverbs 14:29)

3. GOD'S ________________ FOR THE PEOPLE

A. The King's ______________________________

*On that night could not the king sleep, and he commanded to bring the book
of records of the chronicles; and they were read before the king. 2 And it was
found written, that Mordecai had told of Bigthana and Teresh, two of the king's
chamberlains, the keepers of the door, who sought to lay hand on the king
Ahasuerus. 3 And the king said, What honour and dignity hath been done to*

Mordecai for this? Then said the king's servants that ministered unto him, There is nothing done for him. (Esther 6:1–3)

For God is not unrighteous to forget your work and labour of love, which ye have shewed toward his name, in that ye have ministered to the saints, and do minister. (Hebrews 6:10)

B. The King's ______________________________

*And the king said, Who is in the court? Now Haman was come into the outward
court of the king's house, to speak unto the king to hang Mordecai on the gallows
that he had prepared for him. 5 And the king's servants said unto him, Behold,
Haman standeth in the court. And the king said, Let him come in. 6 So Haman
came in. And the king said unto him, What shall be done unto the man whom
the king delighteth to honour? Now Haman thought in his heart, To whom would
the king delight to do honour more than to myself? 7 And Haman answered the
king, For the man whom the king delighteth to honour, 8 Let the royal apparel
be brought which the king useth to wear, and the horse that the king rideth upon,
and the crown royal which is set upon his head: 9 And let this apparel and horse
be delivered to the hand of one of the king's most noble princes, that they may
array the man withal whom the king delighteth to honour, and bring him on
horseback through the street of the city, and proclaim before him, Thus shall it be
done to the man whom the king delighteth to honour. (Esther 6:4–9)*

C. Haman's ______________________________

*Then the king said to Haman, Make haste, and take the apparel and the horse, as
thou hast said, and do even so to Mordecai the Jew, that sitteth at the king's gate:
let nothing fail of all that thou hast spoken. 11 Then took Haman the apparel and
the horse, and arrayed Mordecai, and brought him on horseback through the
street of the city, and proclaimed before him, Thus shall it be done unto the man
whom the king delighteth to honour. (Esther 6:10–11)*

And the afflicted people thou wilt save: but thine eyes are upon the haughty, that thou mayest bring them down. (2 Samuel 22:28)

Pride goeth before destruction, and an haughty spirit before a fall. (Proverbs 16:18)

CONCLUSION

And Mordecai came again to the king's gate. But Haman hasted to his house mourning, and having his head covered. 13 And Haman told Zeresh his wife and all his friends every thing that had befallen him. Then said his wise men and Zeresh his wife unto him, If Mordecai be of the seed of the Jews, before whom thou hast begun to fall, thou shalt not prevail against him, but shalt surely fall before him. 14 And while they were yet talking with him, came the king's chamberlains, and hasted to bring Haman unto the banquet that Esther had prepared. (Esther 6:12–14)

DISCUSSION QUESTIONS

Although we should each have private times in prayer, we see believers praying together throughout Scripture as well. What are some of the benefits you have experienced that come through praying with other believers?

Has there ever been a time that you specifically prayed for wisdom, and the Lord led you to do or say something that you would not have naturally thought of on your own? What kind of decisions require special times of prayer for extra wisdom?

Have there been times in your life when you saw fruit from your labor for Christ come significantly after the initial labor? What are some ways to keep your heart focused toward the Lord during the time of waiting?

WEEK FIVE | DAY ONE

REWARDED

On that night could not the king sleep, and he commanded to bring the book of records of the chronicles; and they were read before the king. And it was found written, that Mordecai had told of Bigthana and Teresh, two of the king's chamberlains, the keepers of the door, who sought to lay hand on the king Ahasuerus. And the king said, What honour and dignity hath been done to Mordecai for this? Then said the king's servants that ministered unto him, There is nothing done for him. (Esther 6:1–3)

When Mordecai discovered a plot to kill the king of Persia, he could have looked the other way. It would have been easy for him to rationalize doing nothing to save the life of a heathen ruler of a foreign empire that had control over the land of Israel and who had caused great suffering to Mordecai's own cousin Esther. Instead, Mordecai promptly responded, sending a warning to the king in time for the plot to be stopped and the king's life spared. Yet Mordecai was not honored or rewarded for his help, despite how important it had been. It was only after some time had passed that the king was reminded of this story, and then he moved to reward Mordecai at just the perfect moment in God's timing.

We do not serve God for the sake of rewards, although His rewards are unfailing. People may ignore, overlook, or dismiss what we do for God, but He never misses even the smallest acts of service. Jesus said, "For whosoever shall give you a cup of water to drink in my name, because ye belong to Christ, verily I say unto you, he shall not lose his reward" (Mark 9:41). We do not need to take action to make sure people know how much we are doing. In fact, doing so ensures that we will not receive any rewards. "Take heed that ye do not your alms before men, to be seen of them: otherwise ye have no reward of your Father which is in heaven" (Matthew 6:1).

Today's Growth Principle: We can trust God to rightly reward us for work done for His glory rather than our own.

REFLECT

What did God say to me as I read today's Scripture and devotion?

RESPOND

How does today's Scripture passage apply to my life? What actions can I take because of what I've learned?

PRAY

Father, it is so easy for me to desire the praise of men. Help me today to serve others for You alone. And thank You for the promise that You see and reward all that I do for You. I pray that You would give me opportunities today to serve in ways others may not even see but that would be for Your glory alone. Amen.

WEEK FIVE | DAY TWO

WALKING BY FAITH

Therefore we are always confident, knowing that, whilst we are at home in the body, we are absent from the Lord: (For we walk by faith, not by sight:) We are confident, I say, and willing rather to be absent from the body, and to be present with the Lord. Wherefore we labour, that, whether present or absent, we may be accepted of him. (2 Corinthians 5:6–9)

We hear much about the importance of faith in the Christian life, and there is a good reason for that: faith is central to every part of that life. It is *essential.* "But without faith it is impossible to please him: for he that cometh to God must believe that he is, and that he is a rewarder of them that diligently seek him" (Hebrews 11:6).

Even so, many people have a distorted view of faith. Faith is not thinking that nothing bad will ever happen. Faith is not believing that God will do anything and everything that we want. Faith is moving ahead in obedience to God even when we do not see exactly what He has in mind.

- Faith is Noah building an ark as God said even though it had never rained.
- Faith is Abraham leaving his home for a place in a foreign country he didn't know.
- Faith is Moses turning his back on the luxury of Egypt for the burden of leading the Israelites through the desert.
- Faith is Peter stepping out of a boat onto stormy seas to walk to Jesus.

Simply put, faith does what God says regardless of how possible or impossible it looks or whether we fully understand His plan. Faith is obedient action in accordance with God's Word, and that kind of faith is pleasing to God.

Today's Growth Principle: Faith that pleases God is not a theoretical, but a practical theology of daily living.

REFLECT

What did God say to me as I read today's Scripture and devotion?

RESPOND

How does today's Scripture passage apply to my life? What actions can I take because of what I've learned?

PRAY

Lord, thank You for being the one I can always put my faith and trust in. Help me to move forward in obedience even when I do not see what You have in mind. Help me to exercise the obedient faith of Noah, Abraham, Moses, and Peter. May my faith today please You, and may I walk by faith in You today. Amen.

WEEK FIVE | DAY THREE

PRAYER AND FASTING

And Jesus rebuked the devil; and he departed out of him: and the child was cured from that very hour. Then came the disciples to Jesus apart, and said, Why could not we cast him out? And Jesus said unto them, Because of your unbelief: for verily I say unto you, If ye have faith as a grain of mustard seed, ye shall say unto this mountain, Remove hence to yonder place; and it shall remove; and nothing shall be impossible unto you. Howbeit this kind goeth not out but by prayer and fasting. (Matthew 17:18–21)

When Jesus came down from the Mount of Transfiguration with Peter, James, and John, He found His other disciples facing a distraught father. He had brought his demon-possessed son in hopes of help, but the disciples had been unable to do anything. Jesus cast the demon out of the boy and sent the rejoicing family on their way. In response to His disciples' question, Jesus talked to them about the importance of faith in seeing God work and how that faith is demonstrated through prayer and fasting. Fasting is sometimes not given the attention that it deserves. It is not a way to prove to God that we deserve His help; rather, it is a way to focus our own hearts and minds in prayer and on our dependance on God.

When Esther was preparing to risk her life going before the king uninvited to plead for her people to be spared, she first assembled a group of people to pray and fast with her. "Go, gather together all the Jews that are present in Shushan, and fast ye for me, and neither eat nor drink three days, night or day: I also and my maidens will fast likewise; and so will I go in unto the king, which is not according to the law: and if I perish, I perish" (Esther 4:16). Casual praying does not produce a powerful answer. It is the intense need that elevates prayer above even necessities like food that successfully deals with the major "this kind" issues we face.

Today's Growth Principle: Our greatest challenges give us an opportunity to see God work in the greatest ways, but we must seek His help.

REFLECT

What did God say to me as I read today's Scripture and devotion?

____

____

____

____

RESPOND

How does today's Scripture passage apply to my life? What actions can I take because of what I've learned?

____

____

____

____

PRAY

Lord, I so easily become self-dependent. Help me today to remember Your sufficiency. Help me to remember my need for You more than for anything else. Help me to see the challenges that You have allowed in my life as opportunities to see Your power work in profound ways. Amen.

WEEK FIVE | DAY FOUR

PRAY FIRST

And, behold, the acts of Asa, first and last, lo, they are written in the book of the kings of Judah and Israel. And Asa in the thirty and ninth year of his reign was diseased in his feet, until his disease was exceeding great: yet in his disease he sought not to the Lord, but to the physicians. And Asa slept with his fathers, and died in the one and fortieth year of his reign. (2 Chronicles 16:11–13)

Asa was one of the better kings Judah had. He loved and worshiped God and worked to stamp out the idolatry and immorality that had become common in the land. Yet after many years of faithful service, when he became ill, Asa did not turn to God for help. He went to doctors instead of and in place of going to God. The doctors were not able to help, and Asa died. We are not told why Asa failed to pray and seek God's help, but we know the results.

Any time that we do not go to God first, we are on the wrong path. There is nothing wrong with getting help from doctors or other experts, but that should always be secondary and come after taking our burdens to the Lord.

We do not pray to let God know we are in need. He is already fully aware of that. We pray out of our love for and faith in Him as our Father. D. L Moody said, "Some people think God does not like to be troubled with our constant coming and asking. The way to trouble God is not to come at all."

Prayer is not meant to be a last resort, but a first response. There are many things that may keep us from going to God. Our pride may deceive us into thinking we do not need His help. Our willfulness may insist on doing things the way we think best rather than trusting Him. Anything that keeps us from prayer is a hindrance that must be removed.

Today's Growth Principle: If our first response to any problem is not prayer, we are not trusting God in the way we should.

REFLECT

What did God say to me as I read today's Scripture and devotion?

RESPOND

How does today's Scripture passage apply to my life? What actions can I take because of what I've learned?

PRAY

Lord, keep my feet on the right path when seeking answers. Remind me to always turn to Your Word and help me to take the actions that I need to keep You first in everything. I commit right now to make You my first response today. Root out any pride that would keep me from going to You for help first. Amen.

WEEK FIVE | DAY FIVE

THE FOUNDATION OF PRAYER

Now therefore, O our God, hear the prayer of thy servant, and his supplications, and cause thy face to shine upon thy sanctuary that is desolate, for the Lord's sake. O my God, incline thine ear, and hear; open thine eyes, and behold our desolations, and the city which is called by thy name: for we do not present our supplications before thee for our righteousnesses, but for thy great mercies. O Lord, hear; O Lord, forgive; O Lord, hearken and do; defer not, for thine own sake, O my God: for thy city and thy people are called by thy name. (Daniel 9:17–19)

The privilege that God gives us to come to Him in prayer is based solely on our relationship with Him, not on anything that we have done to deserve His grace. If we tried to come to Him of our own merit and righteousness, we would never even be allowed into His presence. "And there shall in no wise enter into it any thing that defileth, neither whatsoever worketh abomination, or maketh a lie: but they which are written in the Lamb's book of life" (Revelation 21:27). We don't pray with the right to expect an answer because of our righteousness, but because of His.

Daniel was a man of sterling character who resisted temptation and refused to stop serving God even when it threatened his life. He was a powerful witness in the city of Babylon, showing people that the God of Israel was the true God. Yet he did not point that out to God in his prayer for his people. Instead, he focused on the nature and character of God, and used that as the basis for his appeal.

None of us can ever be worthy on our own, but thanks to grace, that is not what God sees when we come to Him. Paul wrote, "And be found in him, not having mine own righteousness, which is of the law, but that which is through the faith of Christ, the righteousness which is of God by faith" (Philippians 3:9). We who have trusted Christ as our Savior can boldly come to the throne of grace because of the righteousness of Jesus Christ.

Today's Growth Principle: God's righteousness given to us through salvation is the reason we can confidently come to Him in prayer.

REFLECT

What did God say to me as I read today's Scripture and devotion?

RESPOND

How does today's Scripture passage apply to my life? What actions can I take because of what I've learned?

PRAY

Lord, I know that I don't deserve Your grace on my life. Thank you for showering that grace all over my life and reminding me of what You've done. I boldly come before Your throne of grace and confess my constant need for You. Thank you for welcoming me to Your throne by way of Your sacrifice on the cross for me. I need Your mercy and grace today. Amen.

THOU WILT KEEP HIM IN PERFECT PEACE, WHOSE MIND IS STAYED ON THEE: BECAUSE HE TRUSTETH IN THEE.

ISAIAH 26:3

WEEK SIX

THE DELIVERANCE OF GOD

DAY 1: Finished Forever

DAY 2: Enemies Reconciled

DAY 3: Faith that Stands the Test

DAY 4: We Follow Our Focus

DAY 5: Perfect Peace

WEEK SIX | STUDY AND DISCUSSION

THE DELIVERANCE OF GOD

Often in the Christian life, we see God's greatest works after our darkest nights. Those dark nights prepare our hearts for how brightly the light of Christ will shine. In Esther 7, God's glory shone through His people as they were miraculously delivered from Haman's wrath. God's sovereignty was also abundantly clear as He used the gallows Haman had prepared for Mordecai to kill Haman, the enemy of the people of God.

This portion of Esther's life is a great encouragement for anyone who is facing unknowns in life because it reminds us that God does bring deliverance to those who trust in Him.

TEXT

So the king and Haman came to banquet with Esther the queen. 2 And the king said
again unto Esther on the second day at the banquet of wine, What is thy petition,
queen Esther? and it shall be granted thee: and what is thy request? and it shall be
performed, even to the half of the kingdom. 3 Then Esther the queen answered and
said, If I have found favour in thy sight, O king, and if it please the king, let my life
be given me at my petition, and my people at my request: 4 For we are sold, I and my
people, to be destroyed, to be slain, and to perish. But if we had been sold for bondmen
and bondwomen, I had held my tongue, although the enemy could not countervail the
king's damage. 5 Then the king Ahasuerus answered and said unto Esther the queen,
Who is he, and where is he, that durst presume in his heart to do so? 6 And Esther
said, The adversary and enemy is this wicked Haman. Then Haman was afraid before
the king and the queen. 7 And the king arising from the banquet of wine in his wrath
went into the palace garden: and Haman stood up to make request for his life to Esther
the queen; for he saw that there was evil determined against him by the king. 8 Then
the king returned out of the palace garden into the place of the banquet of wine; and
Haman was fallen upon the bed whereon Esther was. Then said the king, Will he force

the queen also before me in the house? As the word went out of king's mouth, they covered Haman's face.
9 And Harbonah, one of the chamberlains, said before the king, Behold also, the gallows fifty cubits high, which Haman had made for Mordecai, who had spoken good for the king, standeth in the house of Haman. Then the king said, Hang him thereon.
10 So they hanged Haman on the gallows that he had prepared for Mordecai. Then was the king's wrath pacified. (Esther 7)

INTRODUCTION

____

____

____

And Mordecai came again to the king's gate. But Haman hasted to his house mourning, and having his head covered.
13 And Haman told Zeresh his wife and all his friends every thing that had befallen him. Then said his wise men and Zeresh his wife unto him, If Mordecai be of the seed of the Jews, before whom thou hast begun to fall, thou shalt not prevail against him, but shalt surely fall before him.
14 And while they were yet talking with him, came the king's chamberlains, and hasted to bring Haman unto the banquet that Esther had prepared. (Esther 6:12–14)

1. THE ______________________ OF ESTHER

So the king and Haman came to banquet with Esther the queen. (Esther 7:1)

Quote: *"When they arrived at Esther's palace apartment, neither the king or Haman knew that Esther was a Jewess. Haman was probably still distressed because of the events of the day, but he composed himself and hoped to enjoy the banquet. . . . Had he known the nationality of the queen, Haman would have either run for his life or fallen on his face and begged the king for mercy."*—**Warren Wiersbe**

A. The King's ______________________

And the king said again unto Esther on the second day at the banquet of wine, What is thy petition, queen Esther? and it shall be granted thee: and what is thy request? and it shall be performed, even to the half of the kingdom. (Esther 7:2)

B. Esther's ______________________________

Then Esther the queen answered and said, If I have found favour in thy sight, O king, and if it please the king... (Esther 7:3)

Trust in the LORD with all thine heart; and lean not unto thine own understanding. 6 In all thy ways acknowledge him, and he shall direct thy paths. (Proverbs 3:5–6)

Thou wilt keep him in perfect peace, whose mind is stayed on thee: because he trusteth in thee. (Isaiah 26:3)

...let my life be given me at my petition, and my people at my request: (Esther 7:3)

And lest I should be exalted above measure through the abundance of the revelations, there was given to me a thorn in the flesh, the messenger of Satan to buffet me, lest I should be exalted above measure. 8 For this thing I besought the Lord thrice, that it might depart from me. 9 And he said unto me, My grace is sufficient for thee: for my strength is made perfect in weakness. Most gladly therefore will I rather glory in my infirmities, that the power of Christ may rest upon me. (2 Corinthians 12:7–9)

C. The Jewish ______________________

For we are sold, I and my people, to be destroyed, to be slain, and to perish.... (Esther 7:4)

If it please the king, let it be written that they may be destroyed: and I will pay ten thousand talents of silver to the hands of those that have the charge of the business, to bring it into the king's treasuries. (Esther 3:9)

2. THE ____________________________ OF HAMAN

A. Haman __________________________

Then the king Ahasuerus answered and said unto Esther the queen, Who is he, and where is he, that durst presume in his heart to do so? 6 And Esther said, The adversary and enemy is this wicked Haman. Then Haman was afraid before the king and the queen. (Esther 7:5–6)

And we know that all things work together for good to them that love God, to them who are the called according to his purpose. (Romans 8:28)

B. Haman ______________________________

And the king arising from the banquet of wine in his wrath went into the palace garden.... (Esther 7:7)

...And Haman stood up to make request for his life to Esther the queen; for he saw that there was evil determined against him by the king. 8 Then the king returned out of the palace garden into the place of the banquet of wine; and Haman was fallen upon the bed whereon Esther was... (Esther 7:7–8)

Quote: *"We do not know the precise form of the couches on which the Persians reclined at table. But it is probable that they were not very different from those used by the Greeks and Romans. Haman, perhaps, at first stood up to beg pardon of Esther; but driven in his extremity to resort to an attitude of the most earnest supplication, he fell prostrate on the couch where the queen was recumbent. The king returning that instant was fired at what seemed an outrage on female modesty."*—**Jamieson, Faussett, and Brown**

...Then said the king, Will he force the queen also before me in the house? As the word went out of king's mouth, they covered Haman's face. (Esther 7:8)

C. Haman ______________________________

And Harbonah, one of the chamberlains, said before the king, Behold also, the gallows fifty cubits high, which Haman had made for Mordecai, who had spoken good for the king, standeth in the house of Haman. Then the king said, Hang him thereon. 10 So they hanged Haman on the gallows that he had prepared for Mordecai. Then was the king's wrath pacified. (Esther 7:9–10)

Recompense to no man evil for evil. Provide things honest in the sight of all men. 18 If it be possible, as much as lieth in you, live peaceably with all men. 19 Dearly beloved, avenge not yourselves, but rather give place unto wrath: for it is written, Vengeance is mine; I will repay, saith the Lord. (Romans 12:17–19)

3. THE ______________________ FOR THE JEWS

A. Mordecai's ______________________

On that day did the king Ahasuerus give the house of Haman the Jews' enemy unto Esther the queen. And Mordecai came before the king; for Esther had told what he was unto her. 2 And the king took off his ring, which he had taken from Haman, and gave it unto Mordecai. And Esther set Mordecai over the house of Haman. (Esther 8:1–2)

For our light affliction, which is but for a moment, worketh for us a far more exceeding and eternal weight of glory; 18 While we look not at the things which are seen, but at the things which are not seen: for the things which are seen are temporal; but the things which are not seen are eternal. (2 Corinthians 4:17–18)

For I reckon that the sufferings of this present time are not worthy to be compared with the glory which shall be revealed in us. (Romans 8:18)

For promotion cometh neither from the east, nor from the west, nor from the south. 7 But God is the judge: he putteth down one, and setteth up another. (Psalm 75:6–7)

Quote: *"God will provide promotions if they are necessary to do His work. You do not need to pull strings, know the right people, bribe the powers that be, or manipulate people to obtain high position.... If you need promotion to do God's work, God will see to it that you get it, and you will obtain it in an honorable way."*—**John G. Butler**

B. The Jews' ______________________

And Esther spake yet again before the king, and fell down at his feet, and besought him with tears to put away the mischief of Haman the Agagite, and his device that he had devised against the Jews. 6 For how can I endure to see the evil that shall come unto my people? or how can I endure to see the destruction of my kindred? (Esther 8:3, 6)

The King Gives Freedom to the Jews

Then the king Ahasuerus said unto Esther the queen and to Mordecai the Jew, Behold, I have given Esther the house of Haman, and him they have hanged upon

*the gallows, because he laid his hand upon the Jews. 8 Write ye also for the Jews,
as it liketh you, in the king's name, and seal it with the king's ring: for the writing
which is written in the king's name, and sealed with the king's ring, may no man
reverse. (Esther 8:7–8)*

The King Allows the Jews to Defend Themselves

*Then were the king's scribes called at that time in the third month, that is, the
month Sivan, on the three and twentieth day thereof; and it was written
according to all that Mordecai commanded unto the Jews, and to the lieutenants,
and the deputies and rulers of the provinces which are from India unto Ethiopia,
an hundred twenty and seven provinces, unto every province according to the
writing thereof, and unto every people after their language, and to the Jews
according to their writing, and according to their language. 10 And he wrote
in the king Ahasuerus' name, and sealed it with the king's ring, and sent letters
by posts on horseback, and riders on mules, camels, and young dromedaries: 11
Wherein the king granted the Jews which were in every city to gather themselves
together, and to stand for their life, to destroy, to slay and to cause to perish, all
the power of the people and province that would assault them, both little ones
and women, and to take the spoil of them for a prey, 12 Upon one day in all
the provinces of king Ahasuerus, namely, upon the thirteenth day of the twelfth
month, which is the month Adar. 13 The copy of the writing for a commandment
to be given in every province was published unto all people, and that the Jews
should be ready against that day to avenge themselves on their enemies. 14 So
the posts that rode upon mules and camels went out, being hastened and pressed
on by the king's commandment. And the decree was given at Shushan the palace.
(Esther 8:9–14)*

C. The Jews' ______________________________

*And Mordecai went out from the presence of the king in royal apparel of blue
and white, and with a great crown of gold, and with a garment of fine linen and
purple: and the city of Shushan rejoiced and was glad. 16 The Jews had light,
and gladness, and joy, and honour. 17 And in every province, and in every city,
whithersoever the king's commandment and his decree came, the Jews had joy
and gladness, a feast and a good day.... (Esther 8:15–17)*

CONCLUSION

...And many of the people of the land became Jews; for the fear of the Jews fell upon them. (Esther 8:17)

DISCUSSION QUESTIONS

Has there ever been a time that you saw the Lord's strength at a point where you felt weak? How was His strength evident to you? What are some of the ways God strengthens us in our weakness?

God gave Esther great wisdom in how she approached the king. What are some things we can learn fromher example for when we need to confront someone, especially someone with authority?

When people wrong us—whether through slander, unfair treatment, manipulation, or clear persecution—how are we tempted to respond? What are some of the natural bad consequences that usually come when we take matters into our own hands? What happens when we release the situation to God and allow Him to take care of it?

NOTES

WEEK SIX | DAY ONE

FINISHED FOREVER

But this man, because he continueth ever, hath an unchangeable priesthood. Wherefore he is able also to save them to the uttermost that come unto God by him, seeing he ever liveth to make intercession for them. For such an high priest became us, who is holy, harmless, undefiled, separate from sinners, and made higher than the heavens; Who needeth not daily, as those high priests, to offer up sacrifice, first for his own sins, and then for the people's: for this he did once, when he offered up himself. (Hebrews 7:24–27)

Jesus is the only Savior because Jesus is the only One who could both be the priest and the sacrifice to atone for our sins. Unlike the priests in the Old Testament era who had to keep offering sacrifices, what Jesus did on the cross was done once and for all, never to be repeated. "When Jesus therefore had received the vinegar, he said, It is finished: and he bowed his head, and gave up the ghost" (John 19:30). His sacrifice was sufficient to pay the price of every sin ever committed. He rose from the dead as evidence of His victory, and He continues forever as our Lord and Savior. This is our confidence and the foundation of our faith. We do not need to doubt His work or His Word—it is eternally settled.

Charles Spurgeon said, "On Calvary's tree He presented Himself a substitute for human guilt, and there He bore the crushing weight of Jehovah's wrath in His own body, on the behalf of all His people. On Him their sins were laid, and He was numbered with the transgressors; and there He, in their stead, suffered what was due to the righteousness of God, and made atonement to divine justice for the sins of His people. This was done, not by many offerings, but by one sacrifice, and that one alone. Jesus offered no other sacrifice: He had never made one before, nor since, nor will He present another sacrifice in the future."

Today's Growth Principle: The precious blood of Jesus paid the price of sin forever for all those who come to Him in faith. His sacrifice for us is the ultimate deliverance.

REFLECT

What did God say to me as I read today's Scripture and devotion?

RESPOND

How does today's Scripture passage apply to my life? What actions can I take because of what I've learned?

PRAY

Thank You, Lord, for Your eternal gift of salvation bought by Your finished work on the cross. Help me never to forget the depth of what You accomplished for the whole world on the cross. Give me a fresh perspective of this to meditate on throughout my day. And, Lord, please give me an opportunity today to share this truth with someone who doesn't know you as Savior. Amen.

WEEK SIX | DAY TWO

ENEMIES RECONCILED

For it pleased the Father that in him should all fulness dwell; And, having made peace through the blood of his cross, by him to reconcile all things unto himself; by him, I say, whether they be things in earth, or things in heaven. And you, that were sometime alienated and enemies in your mind by wicked works, yet now hath he reconciled In the body of his flesh through death, to present you holy and unblameable and unreproveable in his sight: (Colossians 1:19–22)

After America gained independence from England in the Revolutionary War, relations between the two countries remained fraught. Less than forty years after the Treaty of Paris was signed, the War of 1812 saw English troops invade America and burn Washington DC. After that war ended, there were ongoing disputes over boundaries and borders. In the 1840s the slogan "54-40 or fight" (referencing the latitude of the proposed border) gained popularity as a declaration that unless England agreed to recognize all of what was known as the Oregon Territory, which then reached all the way to Alaska as American soil, there would be another war. Considering these years of tensions, it's remarkable that these two adversaries became the closest of allies in the First and Second World War. American support was vital to England's survival as a nation.

Once we were the enemies of God. We were not mostly good people who only needed a little bit of help. We were hopeless sinners utterly dependent on His grace for our salvation. Paul wrote, "Because the carnal mind is enmity against God: for it is not subject to the law of God, neither indeed can be" (Romans 8:7).

Our standing before God was not reversed by a realignment of His needs. It wasn't that once we were His enemies but then He needed us so overlooked our sin. Rather, God made a way for us to become His friends by His atonement for our sin. Through the death of Christ, we were brought into a relationship with God that places us on His side. He has forgiven our sin and made us His friends. We are now part of His family and part of His kingdom.

Today's Growth Principle: God changed everything when He saved us, and we should live every day in light of that difference.

REFLECT

What did God say to me as I read today's Scripture and devotion?

RESPOND

How does today's Scripture passage apply to my life? What actions can I take because of what I've learned?

PRAY

Thank You, Lord, for changing my story from death to life. I don't want to ever forget the sacrifice You made and how I can live free because of Your victory. Thank You for being my closest friend and giving me the opportunity to have a personal relationship with You. Remind me to always show others how they can have that relationship with You as well. Amen.

WEEK SIX | DAY THREE

FAITH THAT STANDS THE TEST

To an inheritance incorruptible, and undefiled, and that fadeth not away, reserved in heaven for you, Who are kept by the power of God through faith unto salvation ready to be revealed in the last time. Wherein ye greatly rejoice, though now for a season, if need be, ye are in heaviness through manifold temptations: That the trial of your faith, being much more precious than of gold that perisheth, though it be tried with fire, might be found unto praise and honour and glory at the appearing of Jesus Christ: (1 Peter 1:4–7)

In April of 1985, Coca-Cola made a startling announcement. After ninety-nine years, they were changing the formula for their popular soft drink. Coke had seen their sales slump, especially compared to Pepsi, and the move to "New Coke" was their effort to compete with changing tastes and customer preferences. The company spent millions of dollars on advertising as they unveiled their plan. The problem was that when it hit the market, people hated it. Coke was deluged with angry calls and letters, urging them to bring back the "real thing." Sales of New Coke were dismal, and just three months later Classic Coke returned to the market. After a few years, New Coke was dropped completely. The product failed the test of the real world.

Our faith is not proven by how much we talk about it or how loudly we proclaim it, but by how it responds to the trials and tests of life. God's promises remain faithful, but sometimes we do not. Real faith, certain faith, precious faith does not melt in the furnace of affliction. Instead, it is shown to be genuine as it stands firm amid the trials.

It is not our strength of will or character that makes faith powerful, but the God in whom we trust. When we rest in His goodness and faithfulness, our faith will stand the test of the real world. David wrote, "Trust in him at all times; ye people, pour out your heart before him: God is a refuge for us. Selah" (Psalm 62:8).

Today's Growth Principle: Because our faith is in God and not ourselves, it can stand firm no matter how severely it is tried.

REFLECT

What did God say to me as I read today's Scripture and devotion?

RESPOND

How does today's Scripture passage apply to my life? What actions can I take because of what I've learned?

PRAY

God, sometimes when trials come into my life, I forget that they are a test of faith. I ask for the strength today to stand in Your truth. I know that I am weak; help me to remember that You are strong. I will continue to pour out my heart to You and allow You to build my faith each day. Thank You for being trustworthy and for being my refuge as Psalm 62 proclaims. Amen.

WEEK SIX | DAY FOUR

WE FOLLOW OUR FOCUS

For which cause we faint not; but though our outward man perish, yet the inward man is renewed day by day. For our light affliction, which is but for a moment, worketh for us a far more exceeding and eternal weight of glory; While we look not at the things which are seen, but at the things which are not seen: for the things which are seen are temporal; but the things which are not seen are eternal. (2 Corinthians 4:16–18)

One of the first lessons most of us had to learn when we were first starting to drive was the importance of keeping our eyes on the road. When you kept focused on where you wanted to go, it wasn't hard to keep the car moving in the right direction. But if you got distracted and turned to watch something you were passing, it wouldn't be long before the car drifted in the direction you were looking. What is true in an automobile is also true in our lives. The things we focus on guide us in the direction we will go. And this is especially true during times of suffering. When we are hurting, it is easy to focus on our problems and on ourselves rather than keeping our focus on Christ.

Paul endured more suffering than most of us can imagine. His fearless preaching of the gospel sparked great opposition. There were enemies who hated Paul and his message so much that they followed him from town to town for the sole purpose of stirring up trouble and forcing him to leave. "But when the Jews of Thessalonica had knowledge that the word of God was preached of Paul at Berea, they came thither also, and stirred up the people" (Acts 17:13). Paul was beaten, imprisoned, falsely accused, shipwrecked, and even stoned.

Yet he remained focused on the eternal rather than the temporal. Rather than focusing on his suffering, he focused on the grace of God and the eternal rewards awaiting him. Maintaining this focus helped Paul remember that what he was doing was worth the sacrifice and investment. "For I reckon that the sufferings of this present time are not worthy to be compared with the glory which shall be revealed in us" (Romans 8:18).

Today's Growth Principle: As we keep our eyes fixed on God through suffering, we'll keep our focus on the eternal.

REFLECT

What did God say to me as I read today's Scripture and devotion?

RESPOND

How does today's Scripture passage apply to my life? What actions can I take because of what I've learned?

PRAY

Lord, focus my heart on the things that honor and please You. I give You my heart to fill with Your desires for me today. Remind me to take my eyes off myself and direct them toward You. You are bigger than my problems. Give me the eternal mindset of Paul, who gave his attention to Your glory and grace rather than his pain and suffering. Please help me to live today with an eternal perspective. Amen.

WEEK SIX | DAY FIVE

PERFECT PEACE

Thou wilt keep him in perfect peace, whose mind is stayed on thee: because he trusteth in thee. Trust ye in the LORD for ever: for in the LORD JEHOVAH is everlasting strength: For he bringeth down them that dwell on high; the lofty city, he layeth it low; he layeth it low, even to the ground; he bringeth it even to the dust. (Isaiah 26:3–5)

In 1555, Nicholas Ridley was sentenced to be burned at the stake in England because of his witness for Christ. On the night before Ridley's execution, his brother offered to remain with him in the prison chamber to be of assistance and comfort. Nicholas Ridley declined the offer and replied that he meant to go to bed and sleep as quietly as ever he did in his life. Because he knew the peace of God, he could rest in the strength of the everlasting arms of his Lord to meet his need.

Most of us will never face a trial of our faith that is quite that severe, yet all of us go through difficult times. During those times, we have the opportunity to fix our minds on God and receive His peace. Or we can do as Peter did when he was walking on the water. It was when he stopped looking at Jesus and began to focus on the winds and waves that Peter began to sink. One of the lovely things about that story is that even when his lack of faith got him in trouble, Peter still believed enough to cry out for help, and Jesus rescued Peter from the water.

We do not need perfect circumstances to have perfect peace. Peace is the promise of Almighty God to His children when we trust in Him. He has given us the promise of Romans 8:28: "And we know that all things work together for good to them that love God, to them who are the called according to his purpose." Peace comes from believing that truth.

Today's Growth Principle: When we lack peace, we should view that as a reminder to focus on God rather than on our circumstances.

REFLECT

What did God say to me as I read today's Scripture and devotion?

RESPOND

How does today's Scripture passage apply to my life? What actions can I take because of what I've learned?

PRAY

Lord, thank You for the promise of peace as I keep my mind focused on You. Help me recognize today as my thoughts stray from what is true, and help me to remember Your promises. Thank You for the reminder that I do not need perfect circumstances to enjoy perfect peace. I trust today in Your promises and in Your sovereignty. Amen.

WHEN IT GOETH WELL WITH THE RIGHTEOUS, THE CITY REJOICETH: AND WHEN THE WICKED PERISH, THERE IS SHOUTING.

PROVERBS 11:10

WEEK SEVEN

FROM MOURNING TO A GOOD DAY

DAY 1: Help from the Heathen

DAY 2: Anchor of the Soul

DAY 3: A Rest to the People of God

DAY 4: A Gift of Thorns

DAY 5: Plan to Remember

WEEK SEVEN | STUDY AND DISCUSSION

FROM MOURNING TO A GOOD DAY

After thwarting the plans of the wicked Haman, the Lord gave the Jews a great reason to celebrate. He delivered the Jews and brought them safety and blessings. To remember the Lord's faithfulness, the Jews created the holiday Purim to celebrate God's deliverance in their lives and to teach the succeeding generations what God had done for them.

We too have a wonderful reason to rejoice and celebrate—God has also saved us! From this portion of Esther, we learn how to celebrate God's salvation. And we see that God can turn even a day of mourning into a day of rejoicing in Him.

TEXT

*Now in the twelfth month, that is, the month Adar, on the thirteenth day of the same,
when the king's commandment and his decree drew near to be put in execution, in
the day that the enemies of the Jews hoped to have power over them, (though it was
turned to the contrary, that the Jews had rule over them that hated them;) 2 The Jews
gathered themselves together in their cities throughout all the provinces of the king
Ahasuerus, to lay hand on such as sought their hurt: and no man could withstand
them; for the fear of them fell upon all people. 3 And all the rulers of the provinces,
and the lieutenants, and the deputies, and officers of the king, helped the Jews; because
the fear of Mordecai fell upon them. 4 For Mordecai was great in the king's house, and
his fame went out throughout all the provinces: for this man Mordecai waxed greater
and greater. 5 Thus the Jews smote all their enemies with the stroke of the sword, and
slaughter, and destruction, and did what they would unto those that hated them. 6
And in Shushan the palace the Jews slew and destroyed five hundred men. 7 And
Parshandatha, and Dalphon, and Aspatha, 8 And Poratha, and Adalia, and Aridatha,
9 And Parmashta, and Arisai, and Aridai, and Vajezatha, 10 The ten sons of Haman*

the son of Hammedatha, the enemy of the Jews, slew they; but on the spoil laid they
not their hand. 11 On that day the number of those that were slain in Shushan the
palace was brought before the king. 12 And the king said unto Esther the queen, The
Jews have slain and destroyed five hundred men in Shushan the palace, and the ten
sons of Haman; what have they done in the rest of the king's provinces? now what is
thy petition? and it shall be granted thee: or what is thy request further? and it shall
be done. 13 Then said Esther, If it please the king, let it be granted to the Jews which
are in Shushan to do to morrow also according unto this day's decree, and let Haman's
ten sons be hanged upon the gallows. 14 And the king commanded it so to be done:
and the decree was given at Shushan; and they hanged Haman's ten sons. 15 For the
Jews that were in Shushan gathered themselves together on the fourteenth day also
of the month Adar, and slew three hundred men at Shushan; but on the prey they
laid not their hand. 16 But the other Jews that were in the king's provinces gathered
themselves together, and stood for their lives, and had rest from their enemies, and
slew of their foes seventy and five thousand, but they laid not their hands on the prey,
17 On the thirteenth day of the month Adar; and on the fourteenth day of the same
rested they, and made it a day of feasting and gladness. 18 But the Jews that were
at Shushan assembled together on the thirteenth day thereof, and on the fourteenth
thereof; and on the fifteenth day of the same they rested, and made it a day of feasting
and gladness. 19 Therefore the Jews of the villages, that dwelt in the unwalled towns,
made the fourteenth day of the month Adar a day of gladness and feasting, and a good
day, and of sending portions one to another. 20 And Mordecai wrote these things, and
sent letters unto all the Jews that were in all the provinces of the king Ahasuerus, both
nigh and far, 21 To stablish this among them, that they should keep the fourteenth day
of the month Adar, and the fifteenth day of the same, yearly, 22 As the days wherein
the Jews rested from their enemies, and the month which was turned unto them
from sorrow to joy, and from mourning into a good day: that they should make them
days of feasting and joy, and of sending portions one to another, and gifts to the poor.
(Esther 9:1–22)

INTRODUCTION

____

____

____

Wherein the king granted the Jews which were in every city to gather themselves together, and to stand for their life, to destroy, to slay, and to cause to perish, all the power of the people and province that would assault them, both little ones and women, and to take the spoil of them for a prey, (Esther 8:11)

And all the rulers of the provinces, and the lieutenants, and the deputies, and officers of the king, helped the Jews; because the fear of Mordecai fell upon them. 4 For Mordecai was great in the king's house, and his fame went out throughout all the provinces: for this man Mordecai waxed greater and greater. (Esther 9:3–4)

1. THE ______________________ OF THE JEWS

A. The King's ____________________

...but on the spoil laid they not their hand. (Esther 9:10)

...but on the prey they laid not their hand. (Esther 9:15)

...but they laid not their hands on the prey. (Esther 9:16)

...now what is thy petition? and it shall be granted thee: or what is thy request further? and it shall be done. (Esther 9:12)

B. The Queen's Final ____________________

Then said Esther, If it please the king, let it be granted to the Jews which are in Shushan to do to morrow also according unto this day's decree, and let Haman's ten sons be hanged upon the gallows. 14 And the king commanded it so to be done: and the decree was given at Shushan; and they hanged Haman's ten sons. (Esther 9:13–14)

Quote: *"Since the Jews were not the aggressors, it means that the ten sons of Haman had taken up arms and attacked the Jews, and all ten of them were slain.*

The bodies of the ten sons were hanged on Haman's gallows as a warning to the enemy.... The sight of ten corpses on Haman's gallows would certainly deter the Persians from attacking the Jews and would result in the saving of lives."
—Warren Wiersbe

For the Jews that were in Shushan gathered themselves together on the fourteenth day also of the month Adar, and slew three hundred men at Shushan; but on the prey they laid not their hand. (Esther 9:15)

C. The Jews ______________________________

But the other Jews that were in the king's provinces gathered themselves together, and stood for their lives, and had rest from their enemies, and slew of their foes seventy and five thousand, but they laid not their hands on the prey, (Esther 9:16)

2. THE ________________________ OF THE JEWS

On the thirteenth day of the month Adar; and on the fourteenth day of the same rested they, and made it a day of feasting and gladness. (Esther 9:17)

A. ______________________

When it goeth well with the righteous, the city rejoiceth: and when the wicked perish, there is shouting. 11 By the blessing of the upright the city is exalted: but it is overthrown by the mouth of the wicked. (Proverbs 11:10–11)

Spiritual Rest in Christ

There remaineth therefore a rest to the people of God. 10 For he that is entered into his rest, he also hath ceased from his own works, as God did from his. (Hebrews 4:9–10)

Physical Rest

And he said unto them, Come ye yourselves apart into a desert place, and rest a while: for there were many coming and going, and they had no leisure so much as to eat. (Mark 6:31)

Quote: *"Fatigue makes cowards of us all."*—**George S. Patton Jr.**

B. ______________________________

And Mordecai wrote these things, and sent letters unto all the Jews that were in all the provinces of the king Ahasuerus, both nigh and far, 21 To stablish this among them, that they should keep the fourteenth day of the month Adar, and the fifteenth day of the same, yearly. (Esther 9:20–21)

Quote: *"The word translated 'feasting' appears twenty times in Esther. Some of the feasting is evil and some is good. The feasting here is good feasting. It is feasting that is celebrating victory over evil. The celebration was indeed a 'good day' (Esther 9:19). Therefore, the feasting was not a drunken orgy but a wholesome celebration. It is fitting to celebrate the victory of good over evil."*
—John Butler

3. THE ____________________ OF THE JEWS

A. A ________________ Day

As the days wherein the Jews rested from their enemies, and the month which was turned unto them from sorrow to joy, and from mourning into a good day: that they should make them days of feasting and joy, and of sending portions one to another, and gifts to the poor. 23 And the Jews undertook to do as they had begun, and as Mordecai had written unto them; 24 Because Haman the son of Hammedatha, the Agagite, the enemy of all the Jews, had devised against the Jews to destroy them, and had cast Pur, that is, the lot, to consume them, and to destroy them; 25 But when Esther came before the king, he commanded by letters that his wicked device, which he devised against the Jews, should return upon his own head, and that he and his sons should be hanged on the gallows. 26 Wherefore they called these days Purim after the name of Pur. Therefore for all the words of this letter, and of that which they had seen concerning this matter, and which had come unto them, 27 The Jews ordained, and took upon them, and upon their seed, and upon all such as joined themselves unto them, so as it should not fail, that they would keep these two days according to their writing, and according to their appointed time every year; 28 And that these days should be remembered and kept throughout every generation, every family, every province, and every city; and that these days of Purim should not fail from among the Jews, nor the memorial of them perish from their seed. 29 Then Esther the queen, the daughter of Abihail, and Mordecai the Jew, wrote with all authority, to confirm this second letter of Purim. 30 And he sent the letters unto all the Jews, to the hundred twenty and seven provinces of the kingdom of Ahasuerus, with words of peace and truth, (Esther 9:22–30)

WHAT MAKES A GOOD HOLIDAY

- Gladness—"from mourning into a good day"
- Feasting—"that they should make them days of feasting and joy"
- Gifts—"and of sending portions one to another"
- Benevolence—"and gifts to the poor."

B. A ______________________________ Day

To stablish this among them, that they should keep the fourteenth day of the month Adar, and the fifteenth day of the same, yearly. (Esther 9:21)

REMEMBER THE TRIAL

Because Haman the son of Hammedatha, the Agagite, the enemy of all the Jews, had devised against the Jews to destroy them, and had cast Pur, that is, the lot, to consume them, and to destroy them; (Esther 9:24)

*To an inheritance incorruptible, and undefiled, and that fadeth not away,
reserved in heaven for you, 5 Who are kept by the power of God through faith
unto salvation ready to be revealed in the last time. 6 Wherein ye greatly rejoice,
though now for a season, if need be, ye are in heaviness through manifold
temptations: 7 That the trial of your faith, being much more precious than of
gold that perisheth, though it be tried with fire, might be found unto praise and
honour and glory at the appearing of Jesus Christ: 8 Whom having not seen, ye
love; in whom, though now ye see him not, yet believing, ye rejoice with joy
unspeakable and full of glory: (1 Peter 1:4–8)*

REMEMBER THE DELIVERANCE

But when Esther came before the king, he commanded by letters that his wicked device, which he devised against the Jews, should return upon his own head, and that he and his sons should be hanged on the gallows. (Esther 9:25)

Quote: *"Even though there was no divine sanction given to this new feast, the Jews determined that it would be celebrated from generation to generation (9:26–28). Note the emphasis on teaching the children the meaning of Purim so that the message of the feast would not be lost in future generations."*—**Warren Wiersbe**

Remember the Safety

Wherefore they called these days Purim after the name of Pur. Therefore for all the words of this letter, and of that which they had seen concerning this matter, and which had come unto them, (Esther 9:26)

Wherein God, willing more abundantly to shew unto the heirs of promise the immutability of his counsel, confirmed it by an oath: 18 That by two immutable things, in which it was impossible for God to lie, we might have a strong consolation, who have fled for refuge to lay hold upon the hope set before us: 19 Which hope we have as an anchor of the soul, both sure and stedfast, and which entereth into that within the veil; (Hebrews 6:17–19)

But God commendeth his love toward us, in that, while we were yet sinners, Christ died for us. 9 Much more then, being now justified by his blood, we shall be saved from wrath through him. (Romans 5:8–9)

For the wages of sin is death; but the gift of God is eternal life through Jesus Christ our Lord. (Romans 6:23)

Remember the Blessings

The Jews ordained, and took upon them, and upon their seed, and upon all such as joined themselves unto them, so as it should not fail, that they would keep these two days according to their writing, and according to their appointed time every year; (Esther 9:27)

CONCLUSION

____

____

____

Remember Your Salvation

Thanks be unto God for his unspeakable gift. (2 Corinthians 9:15)

And let the peace of God rule in your hearts, to the which also ye are called in one body; and be ye thankful. 16 Let the word of Christ dwell in you richly in all wisdom; teaching and admonishing one another in psalms and hymns and spiritual songs, singing with grace in your hearts to the Lord. (Colossians 3:15–16)

Remember Your Blessings

Bless the Lord, O my soul, and forget not all his benefits: 3 Who forgiveth all thine iniquities; who healeth all thy diseases; 4 Who redeemeth thy life from destruction; who crowneth thee with lovingkindness and tender mercies; 5 Who satisfieth thy mouth with good things; so that thy youth is renewed like the eagle's. (Psalm 103:2–5)

DISCUSSION QUESTIONS

Physical fatigue can create a sense of distraction that makes it hard to focus on praising the Lord. In what other ways have you noticed physical fatigue impacting your spiritual life?

____

____

____

What traditions do you already have or could you add to your celebrations—from major holidays to family birthdays and events—to orient the day around praise to the Lord?

____

____

____

How has the Lord used a trial in your life to draw you closer to Him? What are some of the truths God has taught you or blessings He has given you through past seasons of difficulty?natural bad consequences that usually come when we take matters into our own hands? What happens when we release the situation to God and allow Him to take care of it?

____

____

____

WEEK SEVEN | DAY ONE

HELP FROM THE HEATHEN

The Jews gathered themselves together in their cities throughout all the provinces of the king Ahasuerus, to lay hand on such as sought their hurt: and no man could withstand them; for the fear of them fell upon all people. And all the rulers of the provinces, and the lieutenants, and the deputies, and officers of the king, helped the Jews; because the fear of Mordecai fell upon them. For Mordecai was great in the king's house, and his fame went out throughout all the provinces: for this man Mordecai waxed greater and greater. (Esther 9:2–4)

It is nothing new for God's people to have enemies. The Jewish people often faced military threats from foreign nations and plots for their destruction. One of the most serious of these was Haman's plot to use the power of the Persian Empire to destroy the Jews. Through the faith and courage of Mordecai and Esther, God worked to deliver them. At Esther's request, the king granted the Jewish people the right to defend themselves against attacks. That was their legal protection. But God also worked in the hearts of the people, including high government officials, to motivate them to stand up and help the Jews.

God is never perplexed or overwhelmed by any trial or persecution we face. He is fully able to turn the hearts of even those who reject Him most to accomplish His purposes. God does not always deliver His people from physical threats. Throughout the history of the church millions have given their lives as martyrs rather than deny the faith. But God has the tools to ensure His plan is not derailed.

Even when humanly speaking there seems to be no help or hope, we need not fear. Elisha told his servant who was distraught because of the threat of the Syrian army that there was nothing to worry about. "And he answered, Fear not: for they that be with us are more than they that be with them" (2 Kings 6:16).

Today's Growth Principle: God is able to use even those who are against Him to help His children in their time of need.

REFLECT

What did God say to me as I read today's Scripture and devotion?

____

____

____

____

RESPOND

How does today's Scripture passage apply to my life? What actions can I take because of what I've learned?

____

____

____

____

PRAY

God, I praise You that You are not surprised by the trials that come about in my life. Secure me daily in this truth so that I never doubt Your goodness toward me. I will not fear, because You are more powerful than any enemy or bad circumstance that comes along. Keep my mind focused on the fact that You are in control and that You are the best source I can turn to in my time of need. Thank You for taking care of me. Amen.

WEEK SEVEN | DAY TWO

ANCHOR OF THE SOUL

Wherein God, willing more abundantly to shew unto the heirs of promise the immutability of his counsel, confirmed it by an oath: That by two immutable things, in which it was impossible for God to lie, we might have a strong consolation, who have fled for refuge to lay hold upon the hope set before us: Which hope we have as an anchor of the soul, both sure and stedfast, and which entereth into that within the veil; (Hebrews 6:17–19)

In 1979, Sumitomo Industries of Japan completed five years of work when they launched what came to be known as the *Seawise Giant*. Believed to be the longest self-propelled ship ever built, its length was greater than the height of the Empire State Building. The massive tanker was built to be used to transport crude oil across the globe, but its routes had to be carefully planned as it could not fit through the English Channel, the Suez Canal, or the Panama Canal. Fitting the enormous size of the ship, the anchor, which is now on display at the Hong Kong Maritime Museum, weighed thirty-six tons. It was designed that way so that when the anchor was deployed, the ship would remain in place no matter what.

We have been given an even more secure anchor for our faith from our unfailing and unchanging God. He gives us refuge in every storm and a steadfast hope. God does not promise us that storms will not come to our lives. What He promises is to always be there. No matter how dark the night may be or how intense the storm, our hope remains. "But if we hope for that we see not, then do we with patience wait for it" (Romans 8:25).

When the frantic disciples woke Jesus who was sleeping through the storm, their fear made them forget their faith and hope. What they thought of as an insurmountable challenge was simply another opportunity for the Lord to demonstrate both His power over the things of this world and His love and care for them.

Today's Growth Principle: We need never fear that we will be the first person in history to be abandoned by God—He is our anchor.

REFLECT

What did God say to me as I read today's Scripture and devotion?

RESPOND

How does today's Scripture passage apply to my life? What actions can I take because of what I've learned?

PRAY

Lord, thank You for being my anchor and for never abandoning me. Even if the world or everyone I know were to abandon me, I have the assurance that You will never leave me. Remind me of my faith and hope in You when I start to become fearful of the storms around me. Steady my heart and focus it on You. Amen.

WEEK SEVEN | DAY THREE

A REST TO THE PEOPLE OF GOD

For if Jesus had given them rest, then would he not afterward have spoken of another day. There remaineth therefore a rest to the people of God. For he that is entered into his rest, he also hath ceased from his own works, as God did from his. Let us labour therefore to enter into that rest, lest any man fall after the same example of unbelief. (Hebrews 4:8–11)

There is no question that Jesus finished the work of redemption. His death and resurrection provide the final atonement for all who believe. After our salvation, God gives us the incredible privilege of serving Him and being part of His work on this earth. One day we will stand before God and our faithfulness to Him will be weighed. Paul wrote, "For we must all appear before the judgment seat of Christ; that every one may receive the things done in his body, according to that he hath done, whether it be good or bad" (2 Corinthians 5:10).

Yet in this life as we do that work, mindful of the accounting that is to come, we often get tired and grow weary. The world of perfect and eternal rest is waiting for us, but in this life we need God's strength and help to keep going in His work. That rest in this world is promised to us. Jesus said, "Come unto me, all ye that labour and are heavy laden, and I will give you rest. Take my yoke upon you, and learn of me; for I am meek and lowly in heart: and ye shall find rest unto your souls" (Matthew 11:28–29).

Sometimes people talk about being burned out. Sometimes people who have been faithful in service stop doing work for God. The knowledge of the coming rest and the promise of the present rest are enough for us to keep going no matter what.

Today's Growth Principle: God promises to strengthen and give us rest for His work as we rely on His promises and labor in His strength.

REFLECT

What did God say to me as I read today's Scripture and devotion?

RESPOND

How does today's Scripture passage apply to my life? What actions can I take because of what I've learned?

PRAY

Father, thank You for You promises that I can lean on every day for strength. Give me the space to rest when I need it and to stay encouraged to work faithfully for You. Help me to be diligent to stay renewed in You and in Your Word. I want to be able to stand before You one day and be found faithful to Your work. Keep me strengthened for this endeavor. Amen.

WEEK SEVEN | DAY FOUR

THE GIFT OF THORNS

And lest I should be exalted above measure through the abundance of the revelations, there was given to me a thorn in the flesh, the messenger of Satan to buffet me, lest I should be exalted above measure. For this thing I besought the Lord thrice, that it might depart from me. And he said unto me, My grace is sufficient for thee: for my strength is made perfect in weakness. Most gladly therefore will I rather glory in my infirmities, that the power of Christ may rest upon me. (2 Corinthians 12:7–9)

God knows exactly what we need to be most effective in our service to Him. He knows what talents and gifts we have and what will make them productive. He knows how to shape our desires and guide our paths to get us where we need to be. We usually think of His gifts in positive terms. James wrote, "Every good gift and every perfect gift is from above, and cometh down from the Father of lights, with whom is no variableness, neither shadow of turning" (James 1:17). But sometimes the gifts we need the most are not ones we would prefer to receive. Sometimes what we need is a season of suffering, a time of testing, or a thorn in the flesh, like Paul experienced.

We need to be careful in those situations not to rebel against the tools God chooses to use in shaping our lives. While there are times when hardship and loss are the result of our sin, there are also times when they are simply God's preparation for increased fruitfulness in His service.

Jesus said, "Every branch in me that beareth not fruit he taketh away: and every branch that beareth fruit, he purgeth it, that it may bring forth more fruit" (John 15:2). We have to be willing to let go of the things God wants to remove, and we have to be willing to endure the things He knows we need to shape us.

Today's Growth Principle: We must accept God's tools for shaping and pruning our lives so that we can be most effective in our work for Him.

REFLECT

What did God say to me as I read today's Scripture and devotion?

RESPOND

How does today's Scripture passage apply to my life? What actions can I take because of what I've learned?

PRAY

Thank You, Lord, for Your precious gifts to me, including every resource I need to grow in my relationship with You. Shape my desires and guide my path to get me to where You want me to be. I pray for opportunities to exercise the gifts and talents that You have given me. Purge my life of that which isn't pleasing to You and fill it with good fruit that only You can produce. Amen.

WEEK SEVEN | DAY FIVE

PLAN TO REMEMBER

The Jews ordained, and took upon them, and upon their seed, and upon all such as joined themselves unto them, so as it should not fail, that they would keep these two days according to their writing, and according to their appointed time every year; And that these days should be remembered and kept throughout every generation, every family, every province, and every city; and that these days of Purim should not fail from among the Jews, nor the memorial of them perish from their seed. (Esther 9:27–28)

When God used Mordecai and Esther to foil the wicked plot of Haman to destroy the Jewish people throughout the Persian Empire, they rejoiced. It is only right and proper that we give thanks for what God does for us. But that was not all they did. They also established a new celebration, the Feast of Purim, which is still observed today by Jewish people around the world. In synagogues the story of Esther will be read. (A relatively-modern, dating back to the thirteenth century, practice is that children at these celebrations are given noisemakers to drown out the name of Haman every time it is read.) Mordecai established this observance so that the people would not forget what God had done for them in years to come.

Every child of God has received blessings far beyond what we deserve. Salvation alone would be enough to merit a lifetime and then an eternity of gratitude. But God gives us far more than that because of His gracious and loving character. Paul asked, "He that spared not his own Son, but delivered him up for us all, how shall he not with him also freely give us all things?" (Romans 8:32).

We must avoid the trap of thinking somehow we deserve God's blessings. That attitude destroys gratitude and praise very quickly. Instead, we should be reminding ourselves constantly of what God has done, and praising Him to others. "Then was our mouth filled with laughter, and our tongue with singing: then said they among the heathen, The Lord hath done great things for them" (Psalm 126:2).

Today's Growth Principle: Forgetting what God has done for us is easy unless we intentionally plan ways to remind ourselves and others of His grace.

REFLECT

What did God say to me as I read today's Scripture and devotion?

RESPOND

How does today's Scripture passage apply to my life? What actions can I take because of what I've learned?

PRAY

God, I thank You for all that You have done for me. When I look back, it's amazing to see Your handiwork. Lord, let me daily be reminded of how wonderful Your gift of salvation is. I pray for humility to live today in awe of You and Your accomplished work on the cross. Thank You, Lord! Amen.

AND THESE WORDS, WHICH I COMMAND THEE THIS DAY, SHALL BE IN THINE HEART: AND THOU SHALT TEACH THEM DILIGENTLY UNTO THY CHILDREN . . .

DEUTERONOMY 6:6–7

WEEK EIGHT

DECIDING TO REMEMBER

DAY 1: The Things which Are Revealed

DAY 2: The Rejoicing of the Righteous

DAY 3: Living Unashamed

DAY 4: Joy Opens Doors

DAY 5: Generational Impact

WEEK EIGHT | STUDY AND DISCUSSION

DECIDING TO REMEMBER

The book of Esther is a brilliant demonstration of the hand of God in the affairs of men. Unfortunately, we, as humans, often forget the great things the Lord has done for us. As we saw last week, the Jews established the Feast of Purim especially so they would not forget God's deliverance. In this week's study, we focus on how the feast was sustained as a tradition for future generations.

Every generation needs to be taught about God's plan of redemption. One of the ways God has given us to do that is through establishing traditions. Those who serve as spiritual leaders in any capacity should develop and nurture these traditions to preserve a biblical heritage and understanding for others.

TEXT

The Jews ordained, and took upon them, and upon their seed, and upon all such as
joined themselves unto them, so as it should not fail, that they would keep these two
days according to their writing, and according to their appointed time every year;
28 And that these days should be remembered and kept throughout every generation,
every family, every province, and every city; and that these days of Purim should
not fail from among the Jews, nor the memorial of them perish from their seed. 29
Then Esther the queen, the daughter of Abihail, and Mordecai the Jew, wrote with all
authority, to confirm this second letter of Purim. 30 And he sent the letters unto all the
Jews, to the hundred twenty and seven provinces of the kingdom of Ahasuerus, with
words of peace and truth, 31 To confirm these days of Purim in their times appointed,
according as Mordecai the Jew and Esther the queen had enjoined them, and as they
had decreed for themselves and for their seed, the matters of the fastings and their cry.
32 And the decree of Esther confirmed these matters of Purim; and it was written in
the book. 1 And the king Ahasuerus laid a tribute upon the land, and upon the isles
of the sea. 2 And all the acts of his power and of his might, and the declaration of the
greatness of Mordecai, whereunto the king advanced him, are they not written in the

book of the chronicles of the kings of Media and Persia? 3 For Mordecai the Jew was next unto king Ahasuerus, and great among the Jews, and accepted of the multitude of his brethren, seeking the wealth of his people, and speaking peace to all his seed." (Esther 9:27–10:3)

INTRODUCTION

____

____

____

1. ______________________________ DECISION

The Jews ordained, and took upon them, and upon their seed, and upon all such as joined themselves unto them, so as it should not fail, that they would keep these two days according to their writing, and according to their appointed time every year; (Esther 9:27)

A. ______________________________

B. ______________________________

C. ______________________________

For the which cause I also suffer these things: nevertheless I am not ashamed: for I know whom I have believed, and am persuaded that he is able to keep that which I have committed unto him against that day. (2 Timothy 1:12)

Quote: *"It's sad when a nation (or a church) forgets its heroes and the providential events that have kept it alive. How easy it is for a new generation to come along and take for granted the blessings that previous generations struggled and sacrificed to attain! The Jews didn't make that mistake but established the Feast of Purim to remind their children year after year that God had saved Israel from destruction."*—**Warren Wiersbe**

Come, ye children, hearken unto me: I will teach you the fear of the LORD. (Psalm 34:11)

2. ______________________________ DECISION

And that these days should be remembered and kept throughout every generation, every family, every province, and every city; and that these days of Purim should not fail from among the Jews, nor the memorial of them perish from their seed. (Esther 9:28)

A. ______________________________

Therefore, brethren, stand fast, and hold the traditions which ye have been taught, whether by word, or our epistle. (2 Thessalonians 2:15)

Quote: *"Tradition is the living faith of the dead; traditionalism is the dead faith of the living."*—**Jaasoslav Pedikan**

B. ______________________________

And these words, which I command thee this day, shall be in thine heart: 7 And thou shalt teach them diligently unto thy children, and shalt talk of them when thou sittest in thine house, and when thou walkest by the way, and when thou liest down, and when thou risest up. (Deuteronomy 6:6–7)

Quote: *"The consent of the Jewish people to keep Purim was very strong. To this day, the Jews still keep Purim."*—**John G. Butler**

C. ______________________________

Then Esther the queen, the daughter of Abihail, and Mordecai the Jew, wrote with all authority, to confirm this second letter of Purim. 30 And he sent the letters unto all the Jews, to the hundred twenty and seven provinces of the kingdom of Ahasuerus, with words of peace and truth, 31 To confirm these days of Purim in their times appointed, according as Mordecai the Jew and Esther the queen had enjoined them, and as they had decreed for themselves and for their seed, the matters of the fastings and their cry. 32 And the decree of Esther confirmed these matters of Purim; and it was written in the book. (Esther 9:29–32)

Quote: *"This is the same book in which Mordecai's saving deed for the king was recorded."*—**John G. Butler**

The secret things belong unto the LORD our God: but those things which are revealed belong unto us and to our children for ever, that we may do all the words of this law. (Deuteronomy 29:29)

All scripture is given by inspiration of God, and is profitable for doctrine, for reproof, for correction, for instruction in righteousness: 17 That the man of God may be perfect, throughly furnished unto all good works. (2 Timothy 3:16–17)

3. ______________________________ DECISION

A. Leadership Is ____________________________

And the king Ahasuerus laid a tribute upon the land, and upon the isles of the sea. 2 And all the acts of his power and of his might, and the declaration of the greatness of Mordecai, whereunto the king advanced him, are they not written in the book of the chronicles of the kings of Media and Persia? 3 For Mordecai the Jew was next unto king Ahasuerus, and great among the Jews, and accepted of the multitude of his brethren, seeking the wealth of his people, and speaking peace to all his seed. (Esther 10:1–3)

Quote: *"Why did the author mention the new tax program of King Ahasuerus? Some Bible students think that it was Mordecai who engineered this new system of tribute as a substitute for war and plunder as a source of kingdom wealth."*
—Warren Wiersbe

The fear of the LORD is the instruction of wisdom; and before honour is humility. (Proverbs 15:33)

Put not forth thyself in the presence of the king, and stand not in the place of great men: 7 For better it is that it be said unto thee, Come up hither; than that thou shouldest be put lower in the presence of the prince whom thine eyes have seen. (Proverbs 25:6–7)

B. Leadership Is ____________________________

And I will bless them that bless thee, and curse him that curseth thee: and in thee shall all families of the earth be blessed. (Genesis 12:3)

CONCLUSION

For I have received of the Lord that which also I delivered unto you, That the Lord Jesus the same night in which he was betrayed took bread: 24 And when he had given thanks, he brake it, and said, Take, eat: this is my body, which is broken for you: this do in remembrance of me. 25 After the same manner also he took the cup, when he had supped, saying, This cup is the new testament in my blood: this do ye, as oft as ye drink it, in remembrance of me. (1 Corinthians 11:23–25)

DISCUSSION QUESTIONS

What are some traditions you or your family keep that help establish a Christ-focused identity in your home? Is there a tradition you would like to establish?

What are practical, age-appropriate ways parents can pass down God's truth to their children? What are some ways you have seen to be effective? What habits and practices do you want your children to see you consistently practicing personally?

We've mentioned that Mordecai was a humble leader who brought peace and feared the Lord. How do modern leaders show humility, peace, and reverence for the Lord? What are some other characteristics of a godly leader?

NOTES

WEEK EIGHT | DAY ONE

THE THINGS WHICH ARE REVEALED

The secret things belong unto the LORD our God: but those things which are revealed belong unto us and to our children for ever, that we may do all the words of this law. (Deuteronomy 29:29)

Since the knowledge of God is infinite and unlimited, He could never share with us all that He knows. There are many things we will never know or understand in this life, and Christians have been debating certain topics since the days of the first-century church in Jerusalem. We do not need to know what God has not revealed—if we did need that knowledge, He would have given it to us.

This realization makes it even more important that we carefully study, learn, and follow what God *has* shared with us in His Word. The Christian life must be lived by the Bible, or it cannot be lived victoriously and successfully. There are many great books and resources available to us, but none of them compare to the Word of God. That should be our first and most important source of knowledge and guidance. "Wherewithal shall a young man cleanse his way? by taking heed thereto according to thy word" (Psalm 119:9).

We are tempted to take the Bible for granted, particularly if we have been reading and studying it for many years. But familiarity with the Word of God should never steal from us the wondrous gratitude for His revelation to us. The Bible should be a joy and delight to us, and we should never stop pouring it into our hearts and minds.

Thomas Brooks said, "Remember that it is not hasty reading, but serious meditation on holy and heavenly truths, that makes them prove sweet and profitable to the soul. It is not the mere touching of the flower by the bee that gathers honey, but her abiding for a time on the flower that draws out the sweet. It is not he that reads most, but he that meditates most, that will prove to be the choicest, sweetest, wisest and strongest Christian."

Today's Growth Principle: God has given us everything we need to live as He commands in the pages of His Word.

REFLECT

What did God say to me as I read today's Scripture and devotion?

____

____

____

____

RESPOND

How does today's Scripture passage apply to my life? What actions can I take because of what I've learned?

____

____

____

____

PRAY

God, Your knowledge is infinite and unlimited, so I know I can trust that what You have revealed to me is what I need to know for this life. I will trust Your judgment and wisdom. Help me to continue pouring Your Word into my heart and mind. Grant me patience to meditate on Your beautiful love letter to me, the Bible. Amen.

WEEK EIGHT | DAY TWO

THE REJOICING OF THE RIGHTEOUS

In the transgression of an evil man there is a snare: but the righteous doth sing and rejoice. (Proverbs 29:6)

Germany in the early part of the 1600s suffered two huge tragedies. The Thirty Years' War, one of the longest periods of continual war in modern history, swept across Europe as nations struggled for supremacy. In addition, the Bubonic Plague rampaged through the population. Millions perished from war and disease. The German town of Eilenburg had four pastors at the beginning of 1637, but by the end of the year, only one—Martin Rinkart—was left alive.

During that awful year, more than 4,400 people died. Rinkart conducted all of the funerals, sometimes as many as forty or fifty in a single day. In May, his beloved wife died. Yet through all of that suffering and heartbreak, Rinkart retained his faith. He later penned a wonderful hymn of rejoicing that is still sung today.

Now thank we all our God
With hearts and hands and voices;
Who wondrous things hath done,
In whom this world rejoices.

Who, from our mother's arms,
Hath led us on our way,
With countless gifts of love,
And still is ours today.

There are times in all of our lives when things do not go the way we wish that they would. Sickness comes, financial reversal strikes, trouble comes into our homes—we live in a fallen and sinful world, and each of us suffers the consequences of that at times. If you observe people very long you will see that while some go through difficult times and fall apart, others go through the same kinds of difficulties and maintain a strong and vibrant faith. The difference is not in the hardship, but in the faith that chooses how to respond. When we are resting in the love and goodness of God, we can sing and rejoice even in the midst of our trials.

Today's Growth Principle: No matter what our circumstances, the righteousness given us through Christ gives us reason to rejoice.

REFLECT

What did God say to me as I read today's Scripture and devotion?

RESPOND

How does today's Scripture passage apply to my life? What actions can I take because of what I've learned?

PRAY

Lord, no matter what happens in my life, I'm still going to praise You! Your faithfulness in the past has proven to be invaluable to me. Thank You for leading me through past trials and for promising to walk with me through future trials. Remind me to sing and rejoice through the hard times. Amen.

WEEK EIGHT | DAY THREE

LIVING UNASHAMED

But is now made manifest by the appearing of our Saviour Jesus Christ, who hath abolished death, and hath brought life and immortality to light through the gospel: Whereunto I am appointed a preacher, and an apostle, and a teacher of the Gentiles. For the which cause I also suffer these things: nevertheless I am not ashamed: for I know whom I have believed, and am persuaded that he is able to keep that which I have committed unto him against that day. (2 Timothy 1:10–12)

Paul's message was never popular. Even in Damascus immediately after his conversion, Paul's powerful preaching stirred up so much opposition they had to sneak him out of the city to prevent him from being killed. In town after town, Paul experienced riots, opposition, threats, beatings, and he was thrown in prison more than once. He could have concluded that the persecution was a sign that he should change his message. He could have found a safer line of work. He could have stopped speaking the truth. He could have been embarrassed by his "rap sheet." Instead Paul was focused on serving and pleasing the Lord, and because that was his priority, he was not ashamed to suffer for the cause of Christ.

God did not promise us that serving Him would be easy. In fact, Jesus specifically said the opposite. "These things I have spoken unto you, that in me ye might have peace. In the world ye shall have tribulation: but be of good cheer; I have overcome the world" (John 16:33). We do not serve God for the praise and approval of men. We do not serve Him to avoid hardship from the world. We serve Him because He saved us and our love for Him is so great that we cannot do anything else. The world may think or say that we should be ashamed for holding on to biblical beliefs and doctrines, but our response should be to just keep going for God no matter what. We need never be ashamed of faithful service to Him.

Today's Growth Principle: Belief based on the Word of God is not subject to popular opinion or majority vote.

REFLECT

What did God say to me as I read today's Scripture and devotion?

RESPOND

How does today's Scripture passage apply to my life? What actions can I take because of what I've learned?

PRAY

Lord, You did not promise an easy Christian life. But You have promised me peace because You have overcome the world. Thank You for saving me and wanting to have a loving relationship with me. Please give me opportunities to serve You and keep me faithful to what You have called me to do. I love You, God. Amen.

WEEK EIGHT | DAY FOUR

JOY OPENS DOORS

O satisfy us early with thy mercy; that we may rejoice and be glad all our days. Make us glad according to the days wherein thou hast afflicted us, and the years wherein we have seen evil. Let thy work appear unto thy servants, and thy glory unto their children. And let the beauty of the LORD our God be upon us: and establish thou the work of our hands upon us; yea, the work of our hands establish thou it. (Psalm 90:14–17)

The early mission work in China faced many obstacles. Westerners like Hudson Taylor were viewed with extreme suspicion, and their message of the gospel was often rejected without being heard. According to one of the missionaries, a man who lived in the town where their work was located, violently objected to their presence and refused to attend any of the services. Yet after some time had passed, he went the missionary and said, "I want to hear about your religion. I never have heard the words of it, but I have heard the laughter in your house and in the houses of my countrymen who have embraced your faith. And if you have anything that makes people so joyous, I want it."

Of all people, we as Christians have a reason to rejoice regardless of the circumstances of our lives. We have God's unfailing mercy and grace freely given to us, and blessings abundantly far beyond what we deserve. We have the hope provided by the promise of eternal life. We have God even if we have nothing else.

There is always a reason to rejoice. All around us people are hurting. The lost world has no real substitute for joy. They may find temporary diversions and pleasures, but there is no joy apart from God. When they see that joy in our lives, doors will open for us to give them the gospel.

Today's Growth Principle: Until the day God stops giving us His grace and mercy, we have no reason to stop rejoicing.

REFLECT

What did God say to me as I read today's Scripture and devotion?

RESPOND

How does today's Scripture passage apply to my life? What actions can I take because of what I've learned?

PRAY

Jesus, thank You for the ability to have joy in this life. You could have chosen to create us without that ability, but You chose to give us joy. Help me today to find reasons to be joyful so that I will have more opportunities to share the gospel with others. May my joy draw others in to be curious about You. Amen.

WEEK EIGHT | DAY FIVE

GENERATIONAL IMPACT

We will not hide them from their children, shewing to the generation to come the praises of the LORD, and his strength, and his wonderful works that he hath done. For he established a testimony in Jacob, and appointed a law in Israel, which he commanded our fathers, that they should make them known to their children: That the generation to come might know them, even the children which should be born; who should arise and declare them to their children: That they might set their hope in God, and not forget the works of God, but keep his commandments: (Psalm 78:4–7)

All of us have a limited time in this world to make a difference for God. Jesus felt this reality deeply, and it shaped His schedule and ministry. He said, "I must work the works of him that sent me, while it is day: the night cometh, when no man can work" (John 9:4). Wasted days can never be recovered, for when time has past it is gone forever. That truth should lead us not only to diligence, but also to wisdom. This is what Moses prayed in Psalm 90:12, "So teach us to number our days, that we may apply our hearts unto wisdom." We should make sure that the way we are investing the time and talents we have been given will produce a meaningful impact.

There is almost nothing that can have the lasting impact of passing on the truths we have learned and believed to those who come after us. God's plan is that we will live and teach our families in such a way that they will see His truth and want to follow it themselves. "And when thy son asketh thee in time to come, saying, What mean the testimonies, and the statutes, and the judgments, which the LORD our God hath commanded you?" (Deuteronomy 6:20). If our lives in private do not match what we say in public, they will notice. If our faith is real and active in the home, they will notice that as well. The opportunity we have to influence the coming generations must not be missed.

Today's Growth Principle: Our lives should inspire those who know us best to want to love and serve God and to know that He is real.

REFLECT

What did God say to me as I read today's Scripture and devotion?

______

______

______

______

RESPOND

How does today's Scripture passage apply to my life? What actions can I take because of what I've learned?

______

______

______

______

PRAY

Lord, I pray for a genuinely consistent testimony that others can see and be encouraged to love You more. Help me to redeem the time that You have given me today to honor You in every way. Teach me to apply my heart to Your wisdom every day so I can know how to use the opportunities and gifts You have given me to make a meaningful impact. Amen.